# Bosnia and Herzegovina
## History, People, Culture, Travel and Tourism Environment

Author
Samuel Matthews

# Copyright Notice

Copyright © 2017 Global Print Digital
All Rights Reserved

Digital Management Copyright Notice. This Title is not in public domain, it is copyrighted to the original author, and being published by **Global Print Digital**. No other means of reproducing this title is accepted, and none of its content is editable, neither right to commercialize it is accepted, except with the consent of the author or authorized distributor. You must purchase this Title from a vendor who's right is given to sell it, other sources of purchase are not accepted, and accountable for an action against. We are happy that you understood, and being guided by these terms as you proceed. Thank you

First Printing: 2017.

**ISBN:** 978-1-912483-00-6

**Publisher**: Global Print Digital.
Arlington Row, Bibury, Cirencester GL7 5ND
Gloucester
United Kingdom.
Website: www.homeworkoffer.com

# Table of Content

**Abut Bosnia and Herzegovina** ................................................................. 1
   *Introduction* ................................................................................................ 1
   *Land* ........................................................................................................... 3
      Relief ...................................................................................................... 3
      Drainage ................................................................................................ 4
      Climate .................................................................................................. 5
      Plant and animal life ............................................................................ 6
      Demography ......................................................................................... 6

**People and Lifestyle** ...................................................................................... 8
   *Ethnic groups and religions* ........................................................................ 8
   *Languages* ................................................................................................. 10
   *Settlement patterns* ................................................................................. 10
   *Demographic trends* ................................................................................. 12
   *Social Stratification* ................................................................................... 12
   *Gender Roles and Statuses* ....................................................................... 13
   *Marriage, Family, and Relationship* .......................................................... 14
   *Socialization* .............................................................................................. 16
   *Etiquette* ................................................................................................... 17
   *Religion* ..................................................................................................... 20

**Economy and Food** ..................................................................................... 26
   *Agriculture, forestry, and fishing* .............................................................. 27
   *Power and resources* ................................................................................ 28
   *Manufacturing* .......................................................................................... 28
   *Finance, trade, and services* ..................................................................... 28
   *Labour and taxation* ................................................................................. 29
   *Transportation and telecommunications* ................................................ 30
   *Food in Daily Life.* ...................................................................................... 31

**Government and Society** ........................................................................... 34
   *Constitutional framework* ........................................................................ 34
   *Local government* ..................................................................................... 35
   *Justice* ........................................................................................................ 36
   *Political process* ........................................................................................ 36
   *Security* ..................................................................................................... 38
   *Education* .................................................................................................. 39
   *Social Welfare and Change Programs* ..................................................... 40
   *NGO* ........................................................................................................... 40

**Cultural Life** ................................................................................................. 42
   *Cultural milieu* .......................................................................................... 42
   *Cultural Information in of Bosnia and Herzegovina* ............................... 46
   *Number of Cultural Differences in Bosnia-Herzegovina* ........................ 60
   *Daily life and social customs* .................................................................... 66
   *The arts* ..................................................................................................... 67

- Cultural institutions .................................................................................. 68
- Sports and recreation ............................................................................... 68
- Media and publishing ............................................................................... 70

## History .................................................................................................. 71
- Ancient and medieval periods ................................................................... 71
- Ottoman Bosnia ...................................................................................... 77
- Bosnia and Herzegovina under Austro-Hungarian rule ............................... 85
- Bosnia and Herzegovina in the Yugoslav kingdom ..................................... 88
- Bosnia and Herzegovina in communist Yugoslavia ..................................... 90
- Independence and war ............................................................................ 93
- Postwar Bosnia and Herzegovina .............................................................. 96
- Urbanism, Architecture, and the Use of Space .......................................... 100

## Travel and Tourism .............................................................................. 102
- Things to Do .......................................................................................... 104
  - Other things to do ................................................................................ 108
    - Zeljava Airbase .................................................................................. 108
    - Watermills of Jajce ............................................................................. 110
    - Tjentiste War Memorial ...................................................................... 111
    - Stari Most ......................................................................................... 112
    - Kravice Waterfalls .............................................................................. 114
    - Sarajevo Bobsleigh Track .................................................................... 115
    - Sarajevo War Tunnel Museum ............................................................. 117
    - Čolina Kapa Astronomical Observatory ................................................ 118
  - Canyoning ........................................................................................... 120
    - Rafting .............................................................................................. 120
    - Hiking ............................................................................................... 121
    - Mountain biking ................................................................................ 123
- Travel to Bosnia and Herzegovina ........................................................... 123
- Attractions ............................................................................................ 124
- Food and Restaurants ............................................................................ 128
- Shopping and Leisure ............................................................................. 132
- Transportation ...................................................................................... 133
- Airports ................................................................................................ 135
- Travel Tips ............................................................................................ 136
- Visas and Vaccinations ........................................................................... 139
- Weather ............................................................................................... 140
- Holidays and Festivals ............................................................................ 141

# Abut Bosnia and Herzegovina
## Introduction

Bosnia and Herzegovina are a country situated in the western Balkan Peninsula of Europe. The larger region of Bosnia occupies the northern and central parts of the country, and Herzegovina occupies the south and southwest. These historical regions do not correspond with the two autonomous political entities that were established by the internationally brokered Dayton Accords of 1995: the Republika Srpska (Bosnian Serb Republic), located in the north and east, and the Federation of Bosnia and Herzegovina, occupying the western and central areas. The capital of the country is Sarajevo; important regional cities include Mostar and Banja Luka.

The land has often felt the influences of stronger regional powers that have vied for control over it, and these influences have helped to create Bosnia and Herzegovina's characteristically rich ethnic and religious mix. Islam, Orthodox Christianity, and Roman Catholicism are all present, with the three faiths generally corresponding to three major ethnic groups: Bosniaks, Serbs, and Croats, respectively. This multiethnic population, as well as the country's historical and geographic position between Serbia and Croatia, has long made Bosnia and Herzegovina vulnerable to nationalist territorial aspirations.

Ruled by the Ottoman Empire from the 15th century, the region came under the control of Austria-Hungary in 1878 and subsequently played a key role in the outbreak of World War I. In 1918 it was incorporated into the newly created Kingdom of Serbs, Croats, and Slovenes, where it had no formal status of its own. After World War II it became a constituent republic of the Socialist Federal Republic of Yugoslavia. Following the disintegration of that state in 1991, the majority of the population of Bosnia and Herzegovina voted for independence in a 1992 referendum. Much of the country's Serb population, however, opposed independence and boycotted the referendum.

War soon consumed the region, as ethnic nationalists within Bosnia and Herzegovina, with the support of Serbia and Croatia in some cases, tried to take control of territories they claimed as their own. Horrific ethnic cleansing campaigns between 1992 and the end of 1995 killed thousands and violently displaced more than two million people in much of Bosnia and Herzegovina. International intervention into the Bosnian conflict led finally to a peace agreement, the Dayton Accords, in late 1995.

The Dayton agreement ended the war in Bosnia and Herzegovina, but it also established the country as a fragile, highly decentralized, and ethnically divided state in which an international civilian representative remains authorized to impose legislation and to remove domestic officials in order to protect the peace. Although the vast majority of citizens continue to desire sustainable peace, they hold to different ideas about the best configuration of the state, and some even question its future existence.

# Land
Michael Clarke plays a shot as Matt Prior looks on during the Investec Ashes cricket match between England and Australia played at The Kia Oval Cricket Another Cricket Quiz

# Relief
The roughly triangular-shaped Bosnia and Herzegovina is bordered on the north, west, and south by Croatia, on the east by Serbia, on the southeast by Montenegro, and on the southwest by the Adriatic Sea along a narrow extension of the country.

Bosnia and Herzegovina has a largely mountainous terrain. The Dinaric Alps dominate the western border with Croatia, and numerous ranges, including the Kozara, Vlašic, Plješevica, Grmeč, Cincar, and Raduša, run through the country, generally in a northwest-southeast direction. The highest peak, reaching 7,828 feet (2,386 metres), is Maglić, near the border with Montenegro. In the south and southwest is the Karst, a region of arid limestone plateaus that contain caves, potholes, and underground drainage.

The uplands there are often bare and denuded (the result of deforestation and thin soils), but, between the ridges, depressions known as poljes are covered with alluvial soil that is suitable for agriculture. Elevations of more than 6,000 feet (1,800 metres) are common, and the plateaus descend abruptly toward the Adriatic Sea. The coastline, limited to a length of 12 miles (20 km) along the Adriatic Sea, is bounded on both sides by Croatia and contains no natural harbours. In central Bosnia the rocks and soils are less vulnerable to erosion, and the terrain there is characterized by rugged but green and often forested plateaus. In the north, narrow lowlands extend along the Sava River and its tributaries.

## Drainage

The principal rivers are the Sava, a tributary of the Danube that forms the northern boundary with Croatia; the Bosna, Vrbas, and Una, which flow north and empty into the Sava; the Drina, which flows north, forms part of the eastern boundary with Serbia, and is also a tributary of the Sava; and the Neretva, which flows from the southeast but assumes a sharp southwestern flow through the Karst region, continues through Croatia, and empties into the Adriatic Sea. Rivers in the Karst flow largely underground. Numerous glacial lakes dot the landscape. Bosnia and Herzegovina is also rich in natural springs, many of which are tapped for bottled mineral water or for popular thermal health spas.

## Climate

Although situated close to the Mediterranean Sea, Bosnia and Herzegovina is largely cut off from its climatic influence by the Dinaric Alps. The weather in the Bosnia region resembles that of the southern Austrian highlands generally mild, though apt to be bitterly cold in winter. In Banja Luka the coldest month is January, with an average temperature of about 32 °F (0 °C), and the warmest month is July, which averages about 72 °F (22 °C). During January and February Banja Luka receives the least amount of precipitation, and in May and June it experiences the heaviest rainfall.

Herzegovina has more affinity to the Croatian region of Dalmatia, which can be oppressively hot in summer. In Mostar, situated along the Neretva River, the coldest month is January, averaging about 42 °F (6 °C), and the warmest month is July, averaging about 78 °F (26 °C). Mostar experiences a relatively dry season from June to September. The remainder of the year is wet, with the heaviest precipitation between October and January.

## Plant and animal life

About two-fifths of the country is forested with pine, beech, and oak. Fruits are common; among them are grapes, apples, pears, and especially plums. The country's rich and varied wildlife includes bears, wolves, wild pigs, wildcats, chamois (goatlike animals), otters, foxes, badgers, and falcons.

## Demography.

The population was 4,364,574 in 1991. A U.S. estimate of the population in July 2000 was 3,835,777; however, that figure is not reliable as a result of dislocations and deaths from military activity and ethnic cleansing. In 1991, approximately 44 percent of the people were Bosniac, 31 percent were Serb, 17 percent were Croat, 5.5 percent were Yugoslav (of mixed ethnicity), and 2.5 percent were of other ethnicities. Since that time, the Bosniac population has declined and that of the Serbs has risen because of ethnic cleansing by the Serbian army. (The terms "Bosniac" and "Muslim" often are used interchangeably; "Bosniac" refers more explicitly to an ethnicity, to avoid confusion with the term "Muslim," which refers to any follower of the Islamic faith.)

Since 1995, the country has been internally divided into a Bosniac/Croat Federation, which controls 51 percent of the land and whose majority is Bosniac and Croat, and a Serb Republic, which has the other 49 percent and has a Serb majority. Herzegovina, which borders Croatia, has historically had a Croat majority

Samuel Matthews

# People and Lifestyle
## Ethnic groups and religions

Bosnia and Herzegovina is home to members of numerous ethnic groups. The three largest are the Bosniaks, the Serbs, and the Croats. Continuing efforts by the international community to promote the return of persons forcibly displaced during the Bosnian conflict (1992–95) to their original homes, as well as domestic political sensitivities, blocked the conduct of a census well into the 21st century. Nevertheless, it is estimated that Bosniaks constitute more than two-fifths, Serbs roughly one-third, and Croats less than one-fifth of the population.

The three groups share the same South Slav heritage. The major cultural difference between them is that of religious origin or affiliation a difference that may be explained in part by the legacy of the Ottoman Empire, which allowed autonomous religious communities to coexist under its rule. Indeed, "Serb" and "Croat" referred first to the people of two South Slav tribes and then mainly to the people of Serbia and Croatia until the 19th century, when nationalist movements in the Balkans encouraged Bosnians practicing Serbian Orthodoxy to be labeled as Serbs and Bosnians practicing Roman Catholicism to be labeled as Croats.

The idea of a broader Serb or Croat "nation" was appealing to regional leaders who coveted Bosnia and Herzegovina's territory. Serb or Croat nationalism also appealed to educated Bosnians, who were often excluded from high state positions by Bosnia and Herzegovina's imperial rulers. (The Ottoman Empire was succeeded by Austria-Hungary, which took control in 1878.) A sense of nationalism later developed among Bosnian Muslims as well. In the 20th century "Muslim" came to be used as an ethnic, not only religious, identifier; it was replaced in the 1990s by "Bosniak."

The association of religion with national identity has meant that religious identity has remained important. The role of religion within all three populations was elevated by the demise of communism, the revival of nationalism in the wake of Yugoslav disintegration, and the violence of the war. Nevertheless, attendance at church and mosque services continues to be low.

## Languages

The mother tongue of the vast majority is Serbo-Croatian, a term used to describe, collectively, the mutually intelligible languages now known as Serbian, Croatian, or Bosnian, depending on the speaker's ethnic and political affiliation. There are some minor regional variations in pronunciation and vocabulary, but all variations spoken within Bosnia and Herzegovina are more similar to one another than they are to, for example, the speech of Belgrade (Serbia) or Zagreb (Croatia). A Latin and a Cyrillic alphabet exist, and both have been taught in schools and used in the press, but the rise of nationalism in the 1990s prompted a Serb alignment with Cyrillic and a Croat and Bosniak alignment with the Latin alphabet.

## Settlement patterns

More than one-half of the population is rural. The arid plateaus in the southern region are less populated than the more hospitable central and northern zones. Villages are of variable size. Houses are either of an old, small, steep-roofed variety or of a larger, multistoried, modern type.

An urban-rural divide is a significant part of Bosnian culture, with urbanites tending to view villagers as primitives and villagers often being defensive about this view. Young villagers are frequently anxious to move to town. During the 1960s and '70s the urban population almost doubled. This shift particularly affected the economic and industrial centres of Sarajevo, Banja Luka, Zenica, Tuzla, and Mostar, around which sprawling suburbs of apartment blocks were built. Traditional settlement patterns were disrupted by the postindependence war, with the population of many cities swelled by refugees.

Patterns of ethnic distribution before 1992 created an intricate mosaic. Certain areas of the country contained high concentrations of Serb, Croat, or Bosniak inhabitants, while in others there was no overall ethnic majority or only a very small one. Towns were ethnically mixed. Many larger villages also were mixed, although, in some of these, members of different ethnic groups tended to live in different quarters.

Most smaller villages were inhabited by only one group. Much of the violence of the postindependence war had the aim of creating ethnic purity in areas that once had a mixture of peoples. In addition to killing thousands, this ethnic cleansing displaced about half the population of Bosnia and Herzegovina either within its borders or abroad. Estimates suggest that hundreds of thousands of displaced persons eventually returned to their prewar homes, but a significant portion of the displaced population resettled in areas where they were among the majority ethnic group.

## Demographic trends

When it was a part of the Yugoslav federation, Bosnia and Herzegovina had one of the lowest death rates and among the highest live birth rates of Yugoslavia's republics, and its natural rate of increase in population was high in comparison with most of them. By the early 21st century, however, the birth rate had declined, the death rate had climbed, and the natural rate of increase had fallen below zero. The 1992–95 war had radically altered the demographic situation. Of the hundreds of thousands of people displaced during the war, a significant portion of them emigrated.

## Social Stratification

**Classes and Castes.** Before World War II, peasants formed the base of society, with a small upper class composed of government workers, professionals, merchants, and artisans and an even smaller middle class. Under communism, education, party membership, and rapid industrialization offered possibilities for upward mobility. The majority of the people had a comfortable lifestyle. The civil war drastically decreased the overall standard of living, and shortages and inflation have made necessary items unaffordable or unavailable. This situation has created more extreme differences between the rich and the poor, as those who have access to goods can hoard them and sell them for exorbitant rates. In general, the war stripped even the richest citizens of their wealth and left the majority of the population destitute.

**Symbols of Social Stratification.** Under Tito, Yugoslavia had a higher standard of living than did most countries in Eastern Europe; it was not uncommon for people in the cities to have cars, televisions, and other goods and appliances. The upper classes and higher-echelon government workers had more possessions and a higher standard of living. Today, luxuries of any sort are rare.

People generally dress in Western-style clothing. Muslim women can be distinguished by their attire; while they do not wear the full body covering common in other Islamic countries, they usually cover their heads with scarves. Traditional Serbian and Croatian costumes include caps, white blouses, and elaborately embroidered vests; they can be distinguished by the type of embroidery and other small variations. These outfits are worn only for special occasions such as weddings and festivals.

# Gender Roles and Statuses

**Division of Labor by Gender.** Women are responsible for all domestic tasks, including cooking, cleaning, and child rearing. Women who work outside the home generally have lower-paying and lower-status jobs than men do. Since the economic devastation of the civil war, men are more likely to occupy the few jobs that are available, and more women have returned to the traditional roles of housewife and mother. Women are more equally represented in agriculture than they are in other fields, and the majority of elementary schoolteachers are women.

**The Relative Status of Women and Men.** Bosnia has a patriarchal tradition in which women are expected to be subservient to men. Both the Eastern European and Islamic traditions have contributed to this situation. Under Tito's administration, women were given complete civil and political rights. Educational and lifestyle opportunities have increased significantly since that time, although there are still disparities.

## Marriage, Family, and Relationship

**Marriage.** Marriages are not arranged, and love matches are the norm. In 1991, before the civil war, 40 percent of the marriages registered involved ethnically mixed couples. Since that time, mixed marriages have become extremely rare. Despite Muslim sanctioning of polygamy, the custom was practiced in only one region of the country and currently is not practiced at all. It used to be customary for a bride's parents to give the couple a specially woven dowry rug containing the couple's initials and the wedding date.

**Domestic Unit.** The traditional domestic unit often includes parents, grandparents, and young children. This pattern has been disrupted in many cases, as the war forced thousands of people to flee their homes. Many were relocated to refugee camps or other countries, and thousands more were sent to concentration camps. Many mixed families have been torn apart by ethnic hatred, as children and spouses are forced to choose between ethnic affiliation and family ties.

**Inheritance.** Traditionally, inheritance follows a system of primogeniture, passing from the father to the oldest son. Under communism it was legal for women to inherit property.

**Kin Groups.** As in the neighboring Slavic countries, Bosnians traditionally lived in *zadruga,* agricultural communities that ranged from two or three related nuclear families to as many as a hundred. Those communities were patriarchal and hierarchical in organization, with a male *gospodar* as the head. Most important decisions were made communally by the male members. While zadruga no longer exist in their original form, a person's extended family is still considered extremely important, especially in rural areas

## Socialization

**Infant Care.** Tito's government, which encouraged women to work outside the home, established state-run day-care centers for young children.

**Child Rearing and Education.** The current generation of children has witnessed unspeakable atrocities. Children were a prime target of snipers, especially in Sarajevo. Survivors suffer flashbacks, nightmares, and severe depression; in one survey, 90 percent of children surveyed in Sarajevo declared that they did not want to live. The country will be dealing with the effect of the war on these children for years.

Education is free and mandatory for children between the ages of seven and fourteen. There are Muslim schools where students study the Koran and Islamic law in addition to secular subjects and where boys and girls are taught in separate classrooms.

The educational system has been hard hit by the war. Schools were common targets of Serb mortar attacks, and many were forced to close. Some makeshift schools were organized in homes, but many children were left with no access to education. Since 1995, many schools have reopened.

**Higher Education.** The country has universities at Sarajevo, Banja Luka, Tuzla, and Mostar. After the civil war, the university in Mostar split into a Croat university in the western part of the city and a Muslim university in the eastern part.

# Etiquette

Bosnians are known as a friendly, hospitable people. In Muslim houses, it is traditional to remove one's shoes and put on a pair of slippers. Kissing is a common form of greeting for both men and women. Three kisses on alternating cheeks are customary.

Visiting is a common pastime. When entering a home as a guest, one often brings a small present. Hosts are expected to serve a meal or refreshment.

**Dining Etiquette**

Bosnia & Herzegovina identifies with Turkey in many ways and one of Turkey's most significant contributions on Bosnia is in the realm of Turkish Food. Although the Bosnians aren't as outgoing or social as the Turks, dining in Bosnia & Herzegovina is still a social event, which can, on occasion, take hours to finish. It is also important to note what religion your hosts identify with as the Bosniaks are Muslim, but both Croats and Serbs are Christian and this will effect dining and food served. The below information will only cover eating with the Muslim Bosniaks, but be sure to read up on Serbian Dining and Croatian Dining if dining with ethnic Serbs or Croats.

If you're invited into a local's home, arrive on time with some sweets like baklava or have a gift for the family's children if they have any. Dining isn't extraordinarily formal after sitting down; most people, especially in business settings, eat with the knife in the right hand and fork in the left, however some foods are eaten with your hands and pork isn't typically served since few Bosniaks consume pork products. If in doubt on the proper way to eat a particular food, watch those around you. Before the main course is served you'll most likely be given a number of meats, cheeses, and other small appetizers; these are simple and tasty, but don't overeat, they are just the starter.

If the meal is being accompanied by a beverage, never fill your own glass. Your neighbor will fill your glass and you are expected to return the favor. As you finish all your food, feel free to ask for more, this is a compliment to the host. If you're completely done eating (save some room for dessert though), finish all the food on your plate. Often times dessert will be served and many times coffee or tea is offered and expected to be accepted.

If dining out, as the bill comes, the host or inviter should pay for the whole meal. If dining without any locals, summon the waiter or waitress by making eye contact; waving or calling a server over can be considered rude. In regards to tipping at sit down restaurants with a waiter or waitress, round up or tip about 10% of the bill. Small tips to bar tenders are also appreciated, but not necessary.

**Drinks**

Bosnia & Herzegovina's most popular drinks are essentially Turkish in origin. Turkish coffee is a common wake-up for Bosnians, but is drunk throughout the day. Tea, soft drinks, juices, and milk are also widely available.

Despite being a primarily Muslim country, most Bosnians do drink alcohol or at least accept the fact that people around them drink. Two of the more common local drinks are *rakija* and *sljivovica*, which are flavored alcoholic drinks similar to brandy; often times made from plums and grapes. Despite this local specialty, beer is still the most common alcoholic drink, but all popular international beverages are available, including imported beers, wines, and hard liquors.

Generally speaking, the tap water is safe to drink in Bosnia & Herzegovina, but check with locals for any particular regional differences as the Balkan Wars may have contaminated some areas. Also, many people may have troubles adjusting to the local tap water, as it will most certainly be different from what your system is used to.

# Religion

**Religious Beliefs.** Forty percent of the population is Muslim, 31 percent is Eastern Orthodox, 15 percent is Roman Catholic, and 4 percent is Protestant; 10 percent of the people follow other religions. Most of the population is not particularly observant, but religion is an important aspect of national identity. (Islam is associated with the Bosniacs, Eastern Orthodox with the Serbs, and Catholicism with the Croatians.)

Icons, which are images representing Christ, angels, saints, and other holy figures, hold an important place in Orthodox practice and are considered a connection between the earthly and spiritual realms.

**Religious Practitioners.** The central religious figures in Islam are called muezzins, scholars of the Koran who call the faithful to prayer. The Koran is seen as the ultimate authority in the religion. In the Eastern Orthodox religion, priests are the primary religious authorities; they are permitted to marry. The Eastern Orthodox religion does not recognize the authority of the Pope but follows a group of patriarchs who have equal status.

**Rituals and Holy Places.** Mosques are Muslim houses of worship. It is customary to remove one's shoes before entering. The prayer hall has no pews or seats; instead, worshipers kneel on prayer rugs. After Ramadan, people exchange small gifts, visit friends, and have a large family meal.

Eastern Orthodox religious ceremonies are held in elaborate, beautifully designed churches, many of which date back hundreds of years. Each family has a patron saint who is honored once a year in a large celebration called Krsna Slava. A candle is lit in the saint's honor, and special foods are consumed. Christmas (observed 6 and 7 January in the Orthodox Church) is a major holiday. Christmas Eve, called Badnje Vece, is celebrated with a large bonfire in the churchyard and the singing of hymns. In addition to church services, Easter is celebrated by dying eggs and performing traditional kolo dances.

**Death and the Afterlife.** Christians and Muslims mourn the death of a loved one by dressing in black and paying visits to the family of the deceased.

In the Eastern Orthodox tradition, funerals are large, elaborate occasions. In the cemetery, a spread of salads and roasted meats is presented in honor of the deceased; this is repeated a year after the death, at which point the gravestone is placed in the ground. Gravestones often bear photographs as well as inscriptions.

Medicine and Health Care

Tito's government significantly raised the standard of health, eliminating diseases such as typhus, tuberculosis, and whooping cough. More medical workers were trained, facilities were improved, and educational campaigns raised the general awareness of the population regarding health issues.

Many of the nation's health problems today stem from the destruction caused by the civil war. The medical system has been hard hit; facilities have been destroyed, and staffing and supplies are inadequate to deal with the enormous number of casualties. Despite the health workers and aid sent by charitable organizations, these problems continue to plague the health care system and have left it unable to meet even the basic medical needs of the population.

Secular Celebrations

The main secular holidays are New Year's Day, **1 January**; Republic Day, 9 January (25 November in the Federation); Independence Day, 1 March; Day of the Army, 15 April; Labor Day, 1 May; and Victory Day, 4

May. There is an annual Sarajevo Film Festival in late August and a Winter Festival in February and March that is observed with theatrical and musical performances.

## The Arts and Humanities

**Support for the Arts.** Under communism, artists who glorified the state received government funding; most other expression was censored. Since that time, artists have been given more creative freedom, although the religious establishment has used its political power to influence the art that is produced. There is virtually no money from public or private sources to support the arts.

**Literature.** The national literary tradition can be traced back to epic stories that were set to music and passed orally from one generation to the next. While not as prevalent today, this art form was still widely practiced as recently as the 1950s. Contemporary literature is concerned with history and identity politics. The most famous Bosnian writer is Ivo Andric, a Serbian Catholic who was raised in Bosnia and won the Nobel Prize in 1961 for the historical novel Bridge over the Drina.Mesa Selimovic, another novelist, was raised a Muslim but proclaimed himself a Serbian writer. Much of the literature produced in recent years has consisted of nonfiction accounts of the war. One such work is that of Zlata Filipovic, a twelve-year old girl whose diary describes everyday life in besieged Sarajevo.

**Graphic Arts.** Sarajevo and Mostar are well known for the wool rugs and carpets their artisans produce. Turkish influence is evident in the bright colors and geometric designs. Calligraphy and metalwork also reflect traditional Islamic styles. Silk embroidery is a traditional women's art. Contemporary graphic artists have used bullets, shrapnel, broken glass, ash, and other debris to make powerful statements.

The film director Emir Kusturica, a Bosnian with a Muslim background, achieved international acclaim for his 1984 film When Father Went Away on Business, which was nominated for an Academy Award in the United States. Since the civil war, Kusturica's work has been condemned by Muslim authorities, and he has moved to Serbia.

**Performance Arts.** Music in urban areas has strong echoes of the Turkish tradition. Singing is accompanied by the saz, a type of lute. In rural areas, the music draws more on Slavic influences. Ravne pesme is a "flat song" with little variation; ganga is a polyphonic song that sounds like shouting. The main instruments are the shargija (similar to the saz), the diple (a droneless bagpipe), and a wooden flute. Epic poems are performed to the accompaniment of a one-stringed fiddled called a gusle. Sevdalinka songs (from the Turkish word for love) are sentimental melodies usually sung by young women. They are performed throughout Bosnia and Herzegovina and have a strong cultural resonance in the entire country.

There are a variety of folk dances. Some are similar to the Serbian and Croatian forms. The nijemo kolo is a circle dance performed to foot stamping rather than music. There are also different line dances, some performed by men and others by women. Rock 'n' roll and popular dancing are popular and in some cases are replacing the more traditional forms.

The State of the Physical and Social Sciences

The physical and social sciences are virtually nonexistent since the civil war, and there are no funds available for these pursuits. The National and University Library was destroyed by Serbian bombings in 1992 and has not been rebuilt.

Samuel Matthews

# Economy and Food

As a republic of the Yugoslav federation, Bosnia and Herzegovina adhered to the unique economic system known as socialist self-management. In this system, business enterprises, banks, administration, social services, hospitals, and other working bodies were intended to be run by elected workers' councils, which in turn elected the management boards of the bodies. In practice the level of workers' control was extremely variable from enterprise to enterprise, since ordinary workers often were not motivated to participate except in matters such as hiring, firing, and benefits and in any case lacked the necessary time and information to make business decisions. In the 1980s Yugoslavia's large foreign debt and rising inflation lowered the standard of living in Bosnia and Herzegovina.

In the period immediately following the 1991 war in Croatia, Bosnia and Herzegovina's official economy collapsed. Huge increases in the price of oil, falling imports and exports, hyperinflation, shortages of food and medicine, insolvent banks, and unpaid pensions all resulted in a swelling black market, or informal economy. In addition, the 1992–95 war (see Bosnian conflict) caused widespread destruction.

International financial organizations were heavily involved in the postwar reconstruction of the economy. As a result, inflation fell, exports increased and were diversified, and the gross domestic product (GDP) experienced growth, at least until a global financial crisis began in 2008. However, privatization was contentious and remains incomplete. Moreover, the number of workers in the informal sector and the unemployment rate both remain stubbornly high. Remittances from Bosnians working abroad continue to be a significant source of income.

## Agriculture, forestry, and fishing

Bosnia and Herzegovina is a significant agricultural region, with some one-third of its land under cultivation or in pasture. The most fertile soils are in the north, along the Sava River valley. In hillier areas, land is employed for both cultivation and grazing. Principal crops include corn (maize), potatoes, wheat, plums, cabbages, and apples. In Herzegovina and in the more sheltered areas of Bosnia, tobacco is grown. Sheep are the major livestock, although cattle and pigs are raised, and apiculture is practiced. With about two-fifths of the country forested, timber, as well as furniture and other wood products, have been important exports. Fishing potential is increasingly exploited.

## Power and resources

Bosnia and Herzegovina has reserves of iron ore around Banja Luka and in the Kozara Mountains, bauxite near Mostar, and lignite and bituminous coal in the regions around Sarajevo, Zenica, Tuzla, and the Kozara Mountains. Zinc, mercury, and manganese are present in smaller quantities. Forests of pine, beech, and oak provide a source of timber. The country possesses considerable hydroelectric potential; there are several hydroelectric and thermal power plants.

## Manufacturing

Manufacturing historically represented a large part of Bosnia and Herzegovina's economy. In the wake of the war, however, the country struggled to reinvigorate industrial production. Metal manufactures, iron and steel, sawn wood and wood products, food, and textiles are among the products produced in various parts of the country.

## Finance, trade, and services

The Dayton Accords created a largely autonomous central bank, which has sole authority over monetary policy and the issuing of currency. The national currency, the convertible marka (konvertibilna marka; KM), is pegged to the euro. After the war, fiscal consolidation was strong, and most banks are now privately owned. Foreign direct investment was substantial in the early 21st century, but foreign investors faced serious obstacles, including a complex legal and regulatory framework, less than transparent business procedures, and a weak judiciary. Bosnia and Herzegovina's largest trading partners are Croatia, Serbia, Italy, and Germany.

The service sector accounts for more than half of the country's GDP, with retail trade and restaurants being an important component. There have been efforts to revive tourism by attracting visitors to the country's rich cultural heritage sites, gorgeous mountains, and aquamarine rivers.

## Labour and taxation

The largest portion of the labour force is engaged in services, followed respectively by manufacturing and agriculture. Labour unions have been largely fragmented and weak in the postwar economy. Bosnia and Herzegovina's autonomous entities, the Republika Srpska (Bosnian Serb Republic) and the Federation of Bosnia and Herzegovina, have different tax policies. The individual income tax rate in both entities is relatively low. Other taxes include corporate tax, property tax, and value-added tax.

## Transportation and telecommunications

The major obstacle to transportation in Bosnia and Herzegovina has always been the mountainous topography. In addition, much of the transportation infrastructure was destroyed in the postindependence war. The railway system, begun under Austro-Hungarian rule (1878–1918), connects Sarajevo with major towns to the north and with Zagreb (Croatia) and Belgrade (Serbia). Another line runs south from Sarajevo to Mostar and on to Ploče on Croatia's Adriatic coast. However, few lines are direct, and as a result roads of variable quality have in many cases been the preferred means of passenger and freight transportation. Scheduled air services connect Sarajevo with other Balkan capitals, such as Belgrade and Zagreb, as well as with other European and international destinations.

Although Bosnia and Herzegovina has lagged behind its neighbours with regard to citizens' use of telecommunications, the number of cellular phone subscribers increased dramatically during the first decade of the 21st century. During the same period, the number of Internet users grew exponentially.

## Food in Daily Life.

Bosnian food has been influenced by both Turkish and Eastern European cuisine. Grilled meat is popular, as are cabbage-based dishes. *Bosanski lonac* is a cabbage and meat stew. *Cevapcici* are lamb sausages that often are eaten with a flat bread called *somun*. Pastries, both sweet and savory, are common; *burek* and *pida* (layered cheese or meat pies), *zeljanica* (spinach pie), and *sirnica* (cheese pie) are served as main dishes. *Baklava,* a Turkish pastry made of phyllo dough layered with nuts and honey, is a popular dessert, as is an apple cake called *tufahije. Kefir,* a thin yogurt drink, is popular, as are Turkish coffee and a kind of tea called *salep*. Homemade brandy, called *rakija,* is a popular alcoholic drink. Alcohol use is down since the rise in Muslim influence, and in certain areas of the country drinking has been prohibited.

**Food Customs at Ceremonial Occasions.** For Bosnian Muslims, the end of Ramadan (a month of fasting from sunrise to sunset) is celebrated with a large family meal and with Turkish-style sweets and pastries. Both Catholics and Eastern Orthodox believers celebrate Easter with special breads and elaborately decorated eggs. Christmas is an occasion for special family meals among the Christian population.

**Basic Economy.** Bosnia is the second poorest republic of the former Yugoslavia. The agricultural sector, which accounts for 19 percent of the gross domestic product (GDP), does not produce enough

to meet demand, and the country must import food. Industrial production fell 80 percent between 1990 and 1995 because of the civil war, and while it recovered somewhat between 1996 and 1998, the GDP is still significantly lower than it was in 1990. The unemployment rate is between 35 and 40 percent. Bosnia receives large amounts of money in the form of reconstruction assistance and humanitarian aid. In June 1998, a new currency, the convertible mark, replaced the dinar, which had been completely devalued as a result of inflation.

**Land Tenure and Property.** Tito nationalized many of Yugoslavia's farms into collectives. This proved unsuccessful, and he modified the system by giving farmers more control over production. Today, many farms are privately owned. While 90 percent of the country's firms are private, the large government conglomerates are still in place. This has hindered progress toward privatization, as has widespread corruption.

**Commercial Activities.** Crops produced for domestic sale include corn, barley, oats, wheat, potatoes, and fruits. The war has caused severe shortages of food, electricity, and other goods. There is an active black market on which some otherwise unavailable goods can be bought for exorbitant prices.

**Major Industries.** The main industries are mining (coal, iron ore, lead), vehicle assembly, textiles, domestic appliances, oil refining, and military supplies. Much of the production capacity has been damaged or shut down since the early 1990s. There is a negative growth rate of 5 to 10 percent in the country's industries.

**Trade.** The main imports are raw materials, petroleum-based fuels, and consumer goods. The primary exports are machinery, clothing and footwear, and chemicals. Other republics of the former Yugoslavia and Western European nations are the main trading partners. During the war, Serbia and Croatia placed strict restrictions on trade with Bosnia, further damaging the economy.

**Division of Labor.** Under communism, the composition of the workforce shifted from an agricultural base to an industrial one. The more desirable jobs in government often were obtained through connections. Today, as the economy is beginning to recover from the civil war, jobs are difficult to come by in many fields, and connections are still useful.

# Government and Society
## Constitutional framework

The internationally brokered Dayton Accords the peace agreement negotiated in Dayton, Ohio, U.S., in November 1995 established Bosnia and Herzegovina as a state composed of two highly autonomous entities, the Republika Srpska (Bosnian Serb Republic) and the Federation of Bosnia and Herzegovina. The latter is a decentralized federation of Croats and Bosniaks. Each entity has its own legislature and president.

The central institutions of Bosnia and Herzegovina include a directly elected tripartite presidency, which rotates every eight months between one Bosniak, one Serb, and one Croat member. The presidency, as the head of state, appoints a multiethnic Council of Ministers. The chairman of the council, who is appointed by the presidency and approved by the national House of Representatives, serves as the head of government. The parliament is bicameral.

Members are directly elected to the 42-seat lower house (House of Representatives), in which 28 seats are reserved for the Federation and 14 for the Republika Srpska. Members of the upper house (the House of Peoples, with five members from each ethnic group) are chosen by the entity legislatures.

The central institutions of Bosnia and Herzegovina are weak, with the bulk of governmental competencies residing in the two entities. Internationally led efforts to replace the unwieldy and costly constitutional structure of Bosnia and Herzegovina with a more functional one, capable of integrating into the European Union, have been opposed by the country's nationalist leaders.

## Local government

The Federation of Bosnia and Herzegovina is decentralized; it is administratively divided into 10 cantons, which in turn are divided into dozens of municipalities (općine). The Republika Srpska is relatively centralized and is administratively divided into dozens of municipalities (opštine). Citizens of both entities directly elect mayors and representatives to municipal and cantonal assemblies. Arbitration in 1997 established Brčko, in the northeast, as a self-governing special district.

## Justice

The Dayton Accords established the Constitutional Court, which has exclusive jurisdiction to decide any dispute that arises between the entities, between Bosnia and Herzegovina and the entities, or between the institutions of Bosnia and Herzegovina. Three of the nine members of the Constitutional Court are appointed by the president of the European Court of Human Rights; the others are selected by the entities. The State Court, comprising administrative, appellate, and criminal divisions, has jurisdiction over matters regarding national law. Each entity also has its own Supreme Court and lower courts. Since its establishment by the United Nations Security Council in 1993, the International Criminal Tribunal for the Former Yugoslavia has exercised jurisdiction over grave breaches of the Geneva Conventions as well as for war crimes, genocide, and crimes against humanity. In 2002 Bosnia and Herzegovina's national courts gained jurisdiction over cases that did not involve major political and military figures.

## Political process

In 1990 the League of Communists of Yugoslavia fragmented, and multiparty elections were held in each of the country's six constituent republics. In Bosnia and Herzegovina the national parties the Bosniak Party of Democratic Action (Stranka Demokratske Akcije; SDA), the

Serbian Democratic Party (Srpska Demokratska Stranka; SDS), and the Croatian Democratic Union (Hrvatska Demokratska Zajednica; HDZ) formed a tacit electoral coalition.

The three swept the elections for the bicameral parliament and for the seven-member multiethnic presidency, which had been established by constitutional amendment "to allay fears that any one ethnic group would become politically dominant." They attempted to form a multiparty leadership, but their political and territorial ambitions (and those of their powerful patrons in Zagreb [Croatia] and Belgrade [Serbia]) were incompatible.

The parliament failed to pass a single law, and war was stoked by neighbouring nationalists in the spring of 1992. Following the establishment of peace in 1995, the nationalist SDS, HDZ, and SDA continued to win voter support, although other parties that shared nationalist agendas, such as the Serb Alliance of Independent Social Democrats (Stranka Nezavisnih Socijaldemokrata; SNSD) and the Bosniak Party for Bosnia and Herzegovina (Stranka za Bosnu i Hercegovinu; SBiH), gained prominence as well. The institutionalization of ethnicity in the political system has put parties with less ethnocentric agendas, such as the Social Democratic Party

(Socijaldemokratska Partija; SDP), at a disadvantage, though the SDP, too, has gained seats in the parliament and the tripartite presidency.

# Security

The Yugoslav People's Army was designed to repel invasion, and, as part of its strategy, it used the geographically central republic of Bosnia and Herzegovina as a storehouse for armaments and as the site of most military production. Bosnian Serb forces, aided by the Yugoslav People's Army and fighting for a separate Serb state, appropriated most of this weaponry. Elsewhere the Croatian Defense Council, aided by Zagreb, and the (mainly Bosniak) Army of Bosnia and Herzegovina were formed, but cooperation between them soon broke down. The Dayton Accords provided for the state to retain two separate armies, one from the Republika Srpska and the other from the Federation. At the urging of international actors eager to facilitate Bosnia and Herzegovina's integration into Euro-Atlantic structures, the army was unified in 2003. Policing, however, remains decentralized.

Health, welfare, and housing

The health system in Bosnia and Herzegovina is decentralized, which in practice has resulted in inequitable access to health care and uneven levels of service. Informal payments for care are more common than legally mandated co-payments. The poverty rate in rural areas is about twice that of urban areas. In the early 21st century the country ranked toward the bottom of the "high human development" level of the United Nations' Human Development Index, which broadly measures quality of life. It ranked lower than virtually all other European countries, excepting some former Soviet republics.

International programs have helped to rebuild housing stock that was significantly damaged during the postindependence war. In urban areas, most citizens reside in apartments privatized after the war, while those living in rural areas largely reside in private homes.

# Education

Taken when Bosnia and Herzegovina was still part of Yugoslavia, the 1991 census reported that 14 percent of people aged 15 or older were illiterate, with older women accounting for a significant portion of the illiterate population. In independent Bosnia and Herzegovina citizens have good access to educational opportunities, and it is estimated that the adult illiteracy rate fell to about 5 percent by the early 21st century. However, the current fractured educational system, in which students learn according to ethnically coloured, often biased curricula, has had the effect of creating three separate sets of citizens, each unfamiliar with and distrustful of the others. The higher education system is also ethnically divided, although reforms have been launched to meet European higher education standards. The oldest and largest of the country's universities, the University of Sarajevo, was founded in 1949. The Universities of Banja Luka, Tuzla, and Mostar were founded in the 1970s.

## Social Welfare and Change Programs

Tito instituted a welfare system that provided for the poor, the elderly, and the mentally and physically disabled. His government also guaranteed women maternity leave and paid leave when their children were sick.

In independent Bosnia, the Muslim, Croat, and Serbian administrations provide aid for their respective populations. In the 1990s, the majority of the money for social services came from foreign aid organizations rather than from the government.

## NGO

### Nongovernmental Organizations and Other Associations
A number of international humanitarian groups have provided aid to help the country recover from the civil war. One of the largest of these groups is the International Committee of the Red Cross, which, in addition to providing aid and aid workers, investigated Serbian

violations of the Geneva Conventions during the war. Other active groups include Christian Relief, World Vision, the International Medical Corps, and numerous religious, governmental, and humanitarian associations

# Cultural Life
## Cultural milieu

*Diverse European and Turkish influences are felt in the cultural life of Bosnia and Herzegovina. There are considerable variations between traditional and modern and between rural and urban culture as well.*

Bosnian and Herzegovinian culture is heavily influenced by its rich heritage. Cultural diversity is the very core of the country. The population is divided into many groups, but a majority of them are Bosnians, Serbs, and Croats. People of Jewish, Albanian, Romanian, and Turkish descent live peacefully alongside other groups despite differences in their beliefs. Their diversity is also evident in social norms, religious and cultural festivities, music, art, and cuisine.

Regional dances and folk costumes are a treat to watch, and you'll see a lot of them during festivals. Often dancers are linked together either by holding hands or by gripping strings of beads, handkerchiefs, or a piece of each other's clothing as a sign of unity. These performances are accompanied by traditional instruments like flutes, drums, lyres, and violins.

There is strong religious influence in the art and architecture of the country. Among its many attractions are medieval tombstones that can be traced back to the Bosnian Kingdom. Art in the form of early church paintings and carved panels showcase various religious icons of biblical study and saints associated with Catholic and Orthodox churches, synagogues, and mosques. Centuries-old religious buildings are also proof of the diverse culture, along with many other religious landmarks like Gazi Husrev-beg Mosque (Sarajevo), which is the largest Muslim landmark in Bosnia and Herzegovina.

Bosnia and Herzegovina is one of the most diverse countries in former Yugoslavia, and you will feel this almost immediately when you visit. In Bosnia and Herzegovina, three groups make up the greatest percentage of the population: the Bosnians, Croats, and the Serbs. You can also find Jews, Romanian, Albanians, and Turks in Bosnia and Herzegovina. With this rich blend of culture and beliefs, you'll feel steeped in a very old and complex way of life. Enjoy it!

**Home Life in Bosnian Culture**

In the countryside in Bosnia and Herzegovina, families usually live in houses of brick, stone, or wood. Countryside homes were traditionally zadrugas, which were made up of several families living on a common land. Families shared the farming responsibilities to lighten the workload of farming a great deal. Today, you will still find a great community atmosphere in small villages and suburban city regions alike.

Many Bosnians are Muslims, and if you plan home visits during your travels, keep in mind that removing your shoes is regular practice in Muslim households. Slippers are generally provided by the host when you visit Bosnian homes.

**Family Life in Bosnian Culture**

Elders are respected in Bosnian culture and are considered extremely important members of the family. Their opinions and wishes are always handled with the utmost care.

In fact, family life in general may seem more formal, including the relationship between parents and children. Bosnian culture still maintains extended family groups, which means that the grandparents live with their adult children and care for the children while the parents are at work. Godparenting is commonly practiced, and all children are raised with values respecting their older relatives and knowing that they will most likely care for older relatives later on.

Families were affected by the war in the 1990s, which visitors should keep in mind. Some families have been broken up and are now headed by widows after husbands were lost to the conflict. In addition, different areas reached a higher concentration during the war. More people moved into cities from the countryside, where they remain today. Suburban areas became much more heavily populated in the mid-1990s, adding even more personality to these already diverse areas.

## Women and Marriage in Bosnian Culture

Women usually work outside of their homes in cities and large towns. In Bosnia and Herzegovina, women have equal political and economic rights. In many families, women may be more responsible for household tasks like food shopping, household chores, and childcare, particularly in more rural Bosnian regions.

## Food in Bosnian Culture

You'll find that no matter which cuisine you choose to sample, it most likely combines delicious roasted meats, stewed vegetables, and bread in a bevy of combination. Have a traditional Bosnian stew of cabbage and meat, and burek and pida, which are layered meat and cheese pies. Try baklava, a Turkish sweet, to finish off your meal.

**Bosnian Culture Tourist Tips**

In Bosnia and Herzegovina, tipping in bars and restaurants is expected. In smaller restaurants, it's not customary but is always appreciated. Aim for 5-10% of the total.

Use caution when discussing politics. While many Bosnians are both friendly and enthusiastic to talk about any subject, it's recommended that you listen to political opinions and not necessarily voice yours.

# Cultural Information in of Bosnia and Herzegovina

## Cultural Information on Conversations

### Question :
Meeting someone for the first time and I want to make a good impression. What would be good discussion topics?
**Local Perspective:**
People of Bosnia and Herzegovina are very sociable and hospitable. Curiosity often makes them overly straight-forward when encountering newcomers. It is culturally appropriate to ask more personal questions such as "Where are you from?", "Are you married?", "Do you have children?", "What do you do for living?" etc.

It is worthwhile to allocate extra time to establish good communication with your language interpreter. Keep in mind that language interpreting only became an occupation as of 1992. Get to know your interpreter well. He/she is going to be the best indicator of what is currently socially acceptable. This will pay off later on when talking to others.

The power of the collective spirit is still omnipresent. People easily open conversations and you can find yourself involved in a lengthy discussion over something you never thought about before (e.g. historical events dating back 2000 years).

Family, work, sports, music, entertainment, children, local cultural events, good restaurants, and the weather are always good topics when meeting someone on a private basis. Business contacts are more formal.

Humour is always welcome, but it will depend on the person you meet. When meeting someone for the first time, never use topics about religion or nationality. It may offend other people. Humour about marriage, mother-in-laws or politicians socially acceptable.

In overall there are no "forbidden" topics, but it would be recommended to refrain from discussing about military or political events that occurred during the 1992-1996 period. When paying a compliment to a middle-aged man it is advisable to refrain from commenting on his physical appearance. Statements to a man that go against the image of masculinity are definitely offensive and inappropriate.

Tenant and landlord relations are not structured like in Canada. It is recommended that the relationship start on the right foot. It is customary for landlords to come by any time he/she feels like it just to have a social chat.

When visiting someone privately, in a home setting, it is customary to accept coffee, tea, juice, a meal or as offered. Rejection might be seen as a lack of respect for a host.

## Cultural Information : Communication Styles

### Question :
What do I need to know about verbal and non-verbal communications?

**Local Perspective:**
People of Bosnia and Herzegovina do not pay too much attention to personal space. The means of public transportation are usually overcrowded and probably the best place to see what the meaning of personal space is all about. Too much personal space can be viewed as distrust or an authoritarian way of dealing with people.

Eye contact is important and implies honesty and good intentions. At times, you might find it difficult to maintain regular eye contact, as "stereo" talking is common (two or three people talking at the same time).

Touching is very uncommon when meeting someone for the first time. However, shaking hands with both men and women when greeting the person is customary. Men generally do not touch other men unless they know each other very well, or are relatives. Friends are more likely to hug each other and kiss each other on the cheek (Bosniacs and Croats kiss twice, Serbs three times). When it comes to men touching women, a certain level of distance should be kept in the beginning.

Facial expressions are very important and it is customary to have friendly face all the time. There is a proverb "Smile opens a golden gate" that is very appreciated in Bosnia and Herzegovina.

"First three fingers erect" should be avoided at all times within Bosniac and Croat Federation territory; it is a sign of victory welcomed only within Serbian territories. Also the middle finger erect, waiving a pointed index finger and pointing at someone is considered as extremely rude and irresponsible.

Voice is normal, definitely not loud.

## Cultural Information: Display of Emotion

**Question:**
Are public displays of affection, anger or other emotions acceptable?
**Local Perspective:**
It is culturally appropriate and socially acceptable to express strong emotions when amongst people you know. It is very uncommon and not welcomed to express any "heated" emotions amongst people you do not know.

## Cultural Information: Dress, Punctuality & Formality

**Question:**
What should I know about the workplace environment (deadlines, dress, formality, etc.)?
**Local Perspective:**
People tend to judge others based on their dress. It will highly depend on the part of the country you are in. In the urban areas it is more informal whereas in the countryside it will give the entire picture about you.

Dress code is very casual for staff members, and workplaces are more insistent on business attire for management. Your appearance is expected to be clean (especially shoes). During summer months women tend to dress more fashionably and, during winter months, more conservatively and practically.

Communication with staff is welcomed on a first name basis. However, higher management expects to be addressed at the first occasion by using Mr. or Mrs. with the last name until told otherwise. The closer to staff/management you are, it is more common to use first name in everyday communication.

## Cultural Information: Preferred Managerial Qualities

**Question:**
What qualities are most highly regarded in a local superior/manager? How will I know how my staff view me?

**Local Perspective:**
Knowledge, experience, hard work, and dependability are the most highly regarded qualities. Ability to organize, to conduct meetings in a timely manner, and get participants focussed on the agenda are the key measures for quality in the eyes of personnel. An expat would be seen as a role model and judged every step by his/her peers.

If you see that your team members are ready to go the 'extra mile' to meet assigned tasks, then you know you are welcomed. Leadership is also important, and it can be especially useful to introduce daily briefings.

New ideas are welcomed but not as important. Education gives additional weight to an already established relationship, but alone it does not mean a lot (if other qualities are missing).

## Cultural Information: Hierarchy and Decision-making

**Question:**

In the workplace, how are decisions taken and by whom? Is it acceptable to go to my immediate supervisor for answers or feedback?

**Local Perspective:**

All decisions are made by management. Ideas may be generated from various resources (management, other staff), but are carried out by management. Responsibility is usually taken by management, but sometimes they try to share responsibility for bad decisions or failures.

Brainstorming, lateral thinking or "war rooming" methods are not yet common in the public sector. Things are changing slowly inside the private sector.

It is okay to go to your immediate supervisor. Effectiveness of those visits is directly linked to: how often you do that, do you have a good reason or not? It is advisable to keep this to a minimum. It is important to establish yourself as a reliable staff. Very often a staff member will try to resolve everything on his/her own or to discuss issue with your peers. In general "the open door policy" is not yet part of the organizational structure and climate of workforce of Bosnia and Herzegovina.

## Cultural Information: Religion, Class, Ethnicity, & Gender

**Question:**
Briefly describe the local culture's attitudes regarding the following: Gender, Class, Religion and Ethnicity. What impact would the above attitudes have on the workplace?

**Local Perspective:**

**Gender:**

It is a man's world with full respect for a successful woman. Generally speaking, it is harder for a woman to build a career. Women residing within cities have a better status than ones within villages.

**Religion:**

It did not have importance prior to the war. It is probably very important now, especially within rural areas. However, it is less important in mixed areas (areas of mixed ethnicity).

**Class:**

No clear distinction between classes, but it does matter who is who. Antagonism between urban and rural areas is widespread as is prejudice and bias from urban population towards rural. Someone coming from more individually oriented society might find surprising the importance and significance of societal milieu and prestige.

**Ethnicity:**

Ethnicity was always seen like a religion and it is linked to the geographical location and what entity you belong to (ie: Serbian, Croat, Muslim). It is important nowadays more than ever as people are still adjusting to and digesting the outcomes of events during the 1992-1996 period, although it is less important in mixed areas.

Following the main agreements on the establishment of Bosnia and Herzegovina, people generally accept the requirements of ethnically balanced government and its agencies. However the private sector might adhere less to these agreements. Signs of distrust vary from entity to entity and are still visible.

## Cultural Information: Relationship-building

**Question:**
How important is it to establish a personal relationship with a colleague or client before getting to business?
**Local Perspective:**
It is very important to establish friendly relationships with colleagues. That does not necessarily mean personal relationships. It is more a question of mutual trust and respect (e.g. talking about your employment history, projects and company).

To establish a good relationship, a good starting point would be to show knowledge about your work, reliability and dependability as well as a deep interest in the educational background of your colleagues. A good starting point would be an invitation for lunch or coffee. A personal relationship is welcomed if you and the other person are on the same wavelength and understand each other.

## Cultural Information: Privileges and Favoritism

### Question:
Would a colleague or employee expect special privileges or considerations given our personal relationship or friendship

### Local Perspective:
It is customary to expect 'special' treatment if personal relationship/friendship is present. Usually it is expected to have his/her family member to be hired even within the same office. Unfortunately this became a practice of many international NGOs offices and this has reinforced the acceptability of this practice.

It is common, both in the private and public sectors, that those hiring will give special consideration to people they know who are in need. This is particularly true where no obvious qualified applicants are available. It is also more frequent within smaller cities than in main centres.

## Cultural Information: Conflicts in the Workplace

**Question:**
I have a work-related problem with a colleague. Do I confront him or her directly? Privately or publicly?

**Local Perspective:**
Personal interactions inside the workforce follow the principles of communist ideology. Work related problems of big scale are sorted out by the principles of a worker's union's philosophy unless one of the workers had a relative or friend higher up to step in and help resolve the conflict.

The majority of people apply a strategy of compromise. Colleagues typically confront each other directly, spelling out the issue immediately.

## Cultural Information: Motivating Local Colleagues

**Question:**
What motivates my local colleagues to perform well on the job?

**Local Perspective:**
Nowadays, one would be considered quite successful to have a well paying job in Bosnia and Herzegovina. People no longer believe so much in commitment to their organization since the break-up of the Former Yugoslavia.

Recognition for a job well done is definitely important and seen as a good motivator; especially if it comes from a foreigner.

## Cultural Information: Recommended Books, Films & Foods

**Question:**
To help me learn more about the local culture(s), please recommend: books, films, television shows, foods and web sites.

**Local Perspective:**
*Movies:* Perfect Circle by Ademir Kenovic; the first post-war feature; a multi-award winner; No Man's Land by Denis Tanovic; pre-eminent a Bosnian movie; Walter Defends Sarajevo by Hajrudin Krvavac - traditional action thriller extolling wartime (WWII) resistance; When Father Was Away on Business by Emir Kusturica and Tito's Break with Stalin. Finally, The Scent of Quinces by Mirza Idrizovic—the story of close-knit Muslim family in the early days of the World War Two.

*Books: Stone Sleeper*, the poetry of Mak Dizdar about the Bosnian landscape, history, unique and mysterious mediaeval tombstones that lie scattered across the Bosnian countryside; *As Long as Sarajevo Exists* by Kemal Kurspahic, the memoir by the editor-in-chief of Oslobodjenje from 1991 to 1995 presenting survival of an operative civil society in Sarajevo under siege; and *Balkan Babel* by Sabrina Ramet, describing political developments of the 1980s, the press, rock music, the Catholic and Serbian Orthodox Churches, Islam, the run-up to war in Croatia, the emergence of an independent Slovenia and Macedonia, the Bosnian war and international responses to it.

Also, *Bosnia: a Short History* by Noel Malcolm, covers the whole history of Bosnia, from the end of the Roman Empire to the Dayton Accords. Likewise, *Bosnia: A Cultural History* by Ivan Lovrenovic, foreword by Ammiel Alcalay, a brief survey of the cultural history of Bosnia and Herzegovina. Finally, *The Death of Yugoslavia* by Laura Silber and Allan Little; covers the period 1986 to 1995; written to accompany a BBC TV series and *Black Lamb and Grey Falcon: A Journey Through Yugoslavia* by Rebecca West, who writes about the history, politics and culture of the region.

*Music:* Ivan Kalcina, famous guitar player; Kemal Monteno, a singer whose lirics and music best describe Sarajevo in his song "Sarajevo-Ljubavi moja" during the Winter Olympic Games.

*Useful internet links:* www.bosnia.org.uk; www.saray.net; www.osce.org; www.bhembassy.org; www.fbihvlada.gov.ba; www.utic.net.ba

## Cultural Information: In-country Activities
**Question:**

# When in this country, I want to learn more about the culture(s) and people. What activities can you recommend?

**Local Perspective:**
Before starting any trip to any locations in ex-Yugoslavia, you must always remember the two main dangers in Bosnia and Herzegovina: the roads and the mines.

The winter season is a good opportunity to explore the repertoire of six theatres in downtown Sarajevo. Don't miss the opportunity to visit museums, such as the National Museum in Sarajevo and its two Millennium long expositions. Take a walk in the old town (stari grad) Bascarsija. It is very interesting with its small and narrow streets and bazaars with religious buildings all located within a short distance. Also good for food.

You may discover famous or less well-known lakes such as the Jablanicko, Boracko, Ramsko, to name only few. In fact, each municipality has its own lovely lake. All are beautiful in every season, and some are equipped for fishing, canoeing, sailing, or even water skiing and jet-skiing (preferably in summer).

Bridges are also very important part of Bosnian & Herzegovinian culture. They were built for crossing the rivers or to expand the cities. Some of those bridges are renowned, such as the Visegrad, one on the

Drina River, or the one in Sarajevo where Archduke Franz Ferdinand was assassinated in 1914. There is also the Arskanagic Bridge over the Trebisnjica River. Some are very ancient, as the Rimski Most (Roman Bridge) south of Sarajevo and the most famous of all, the Mostar's 'Stari Most' (Old Bridge) that was destroyed, unfortunately, during the war. It is now in the process of reconstruction.

There are in total 38 restaurants in Sarajevo mostly located in downtown. There are a lot of delicious Balkan specialities, halfway between the Occidental and Middle Eastern cooking. There are two Chinese restaurants and Taj Mahal as well. Don't miss 'cevapcici', 'burek', 'dolmes', 'bamia' and all sorts of oriental pastries.

The best vineyards are located in the Herzegovina region, where southern sunshine allows for perfect grape ripening.

Newspapers, weekly magazines, TV, café-bars are good things to start with, of course with the assistance of your language assistant. Usually your peers and or your staff will give you a good source of information assuming that you share the same interest (you work in the same field or expertise).

# Number of Cultural Differences in Bosnia-Herzegovina

## Coffee Life

In America, going out for coffee is a quick and easy task. Maybe you'll go on a coffee date and order a caramel macchiato and your date will get milk and sugar with coffee flavoring. But typically getting coffee in the United States is run in, order, and rush out to other tasks on your to do list for the day. In Bosnia-Herzegovina, this is not the case. Walking down any street in Bosnia, you will find multiple cafes lined up beside each other, all filled with people. When Bosnians feel like coffee, they don't care where they stop; though they may have a favorite place or a favorite drink, it isn't always a priority.

Going for coffee is social time for Bosnians, and you'll rarely see a person sitting by themselves in a cafe. Bosnians can sit for hours with their friends, talking about the news, daily gossip, or whatever information passed their ears that week, with a bosanska kafa situated in front of them.

When Americans first arrive in Bosnia, it may be a bit of a struggle adjusting to sitting down for coffee for so long, but soon they'll find themselves boasting the amount of hours they've sat in those cafe chairs, conversing or working on small projects. Coffee in Bosnia is nearly sacred and coffee time is never skipped. It's a wonderful part of

Bosnian life that makes you truly come to appreciate the country and culture, as well as just sit down and enjoy the company around you.

## Public Transportation

Public transportation wouldn't seem like an obvious cultural difference to the naked eye. There are buses, trams, and trolleys, just like many American cities, however, within this transportation system lies the true cultural differences. In America, it's all about personal space; don't touch anyone else, keep your belongings with you at all times, and just mind your own business. In some ways, Bosnia is quite similar in that sense. However, taking public transportation can also mean long conversations with an old man who visited America when he was younger or a woman letting you place your shopping bags on her lap while you stand.

When someone takes public transportation in Bosnia, especially at busy hours like when school and work get out, there is no such thing as personal space. Bodies are pressed against the windows of transport vehicles and windows are opened to give people air, as the driver allows passengers to squeeze on and off. The major public transportation company (GRAS) checks for tickets, but more often than not people just jump on and off without a ticket. Many people do not own cars in Bosnia, so public transportation is the key way to get around the city for most.

## Sickness

Being sick in Bosnia is a completely new experience. Instead of simply taking an ibuprofen and drinking tea, there is a whole long list of remedies to cure your illness, not to mention a long list of causes. You leave the window open, you'll catch the draft. Sitting on concrete as a woman is a big no-no as it'll freeze your ovaries and you won't be able to have children. Having pains while you're pregnant? Cut up onions and place them on your back. Maybe you caught a little cold because you forgot to wear socks, so you should make tea and utilize the tea bags by placing them on your eyes. You might have a bit of a headache due to your kidneys being infected from not wearing an undershirt. Bosnian mothers will baby you until you are sure you are better, but take every precaution to make sure your health stays at the top of its game.

## Gender Roles

Bosnia is incredibly traditional when it comes to gender roles. In American society, feminism is a large movement, trying to prove that women belong in certain roles the same as men. While women work in many different fields in Bosnia, in home life, it's quite separated.

The woman of the house is the one who cooks and cleans, even if she holds a steady job, while the man works on outdoor chores or simply lays on the couch watching sports when he isn't working. For newer generations, the roles are changing for the most part; however, families that were getting started during the Bosnian War remain more traditional and handfuls of new generation families still cling to old traditions. Gender roles in sports are quite segregated.

There are plenty of sports open to males, such as the nation's most popular sport soccer, and even swimming and skating too. But joining sports for women is much more difficult and there is less to choose from. In fact, a woman simply going to a fitness center is seen as strange and will surely provoke odd looks. With time it is becoming more common to see both genders participating in sports, but for now the roles remain overall traditional in most respects.

## Stray Animals

After the Bosnian War, homes were destroyed and left in disarray and pets were included in the chaotic mess that was left standing. Since then stray dogs and cats can be found on every street, often scrounging through garbage cans for food. Some Bosnians set out food for stray animals, such as scraps from their meals or specifically bought cans of tuna for the kittens living underneath garbage barrels outside their back door. Due to the fact that many of the animals were previously owned and raised as pets, they are often kind and don't bother strangers without being provoked. If you decide to pet the dogs or cats, just be sure to wash your hands afterwards; you'll notice that almost any animal seems to be in search of some love!

Typically, Bosnians are more aggressive towards animals, shooing them away or kicking them if they get too close. Bosnian woman sometimes chase them away with brooms and men often just hit the dogs if they are being bothersome. Be extra aware of dogs in the winter when food is hard to come by, but the majority of the time stray animals remain kind and apathetic.

## Eating

**Eating in Bosnia-Herzegovina is a treat**. Being a big eater is something you will never have to be ashamed of, instead you will begin to take pride in it. If you eat everything you are served when visiting someone's home, the host will automatically serve you more food, believing you are still hungry. To avoid this, leave a bite or two on your plate, because if you say "Nisam gladna!" (the feminine translation of "I'm not hungry") they simply won't believe it. Every social event contains food, whether it be a traditional dish, such as *burek*, *cevapi*, *musaka*, or *pita*, or just desserts.

Coffee joins this gathering rule as well. Always remember: coffee and food will be served to you, regardless of if you are thirsty or hungry.

## Walking

Although public transportation is an easy and attainable option to get around, more often than not, people walk. Sometimes public transportation can be unreliable, if GRAS goes on strike or the transport is merely off schedule, walking is the number one way to be sure you can get from one place to another on time. Many people wear flat shoes to walk on cobble stones and uneven pavement, however there are the few women who have mastered wearing heels down in Old Town, which is nothing but uneven walkways. Walking is also the perfect way to see the best places in Bosnia too. All the cities have hidden treasures, tucked away down alleyways or up a hill, that can only be reached by foot.

# Daily life and social customs

Family ties are strong, and friendship and neighbourhood networks are well developed. Great value is placed on hospitality, spontaneity, and the gifts of storytelling and wit. Summer activities include strolling on town korza (promenades), and throughout the year popular meeting places are kafane (traditional coffeehouses) and kafići (modern café-bars). Bosnian cuisine is a matter of pride and displays its Turkish influence in stuffed vegetables, coffee, and sweet cakes of the baklava type, as well as in the national dish of ćevapi, or ćevapčići. These small rolls of seasoned ground meat, typically a mixture of beef and lamb, are grilled and usually served in a bread pocket. The plums that grow in the country are often made into thick jam or slivovitz, a popular brandy.

## The arts

During the 1970s Sarajevo, with a less repressive atmosphere than that of the Yugoslav capital of Belgrade (now in Serbia), gave rise to a dissident rock-and-roll culture. The most popular band of the time, Bijelo Dugme ("White Button"), enjoyed a large following throughout the country. The city has produced other popular musical groups and artists, such as Zabranjeno Pušenje, Divlje Jagode, Elvis J. Kurtović, and Crvena Jabuka. International artists toured the country during the 1992–95 war in the service of humanitarian causes, and they continue to do so, adding to a strong domestic tradition of musical and cultural performance. Folk songs remain popular and well-known.

Sarajevo enjoys an active literary culture as well, with a number of publishing houses releasing contemporary and classic writing from the region. Popular writers include Amila Buturović, Semezdin Mehmedinović, Meša Selimović, and Fahrudin Zilkić. Ivo Andrić, born in Dolac, Bosnia, received the 1961 Nobel Prize for Literature. Andrić's novels, such as Na Drini ćuprija (1945; The Bridge on the Drina), are concerned with the history of Bosnia.

In the Yugoslav era Sarajevo was an important film centre, gaining international renown through the work of director Emir Kusturica, whose films depict the private face of Yugoslavia's history. His Sječaš li se Dolly Bell? (Do You Remember Dolly Bell?) won the Golden Lion award at the 1981 Venice Film Festival. Danis Tanović won an Oscar in 2002 for his film No Man's Land, about human relationships during the 1992–95 war.

## Cultural institutions

The National Museum (Zemaljski Muzej) in Sarajevo offers items from the Neolithic Period (New Stone Age), Roman findings, medieval tombstones (stećci), the Jewish illuminated manuscript known as the Sarajevo Haggadah, and folk costumes. Sarajevo's National Theatre hosts productions by local, regional, and international groups. The Italian opera star Luciano Pavarotti lent his talent to raise funds for the Pavarotti Music Centre in Mostar, an institution that offers courses in music, filmmaking, photography, and acting.

## Sports and recreation

Bosnians, like many Europeans, share a passion for football (soccer). The country fields dozens of professional and semiprofessional teams, and virtually no Bosnian village lacks a field and a few players willing to populate it. The civil war of the 1990s caused the Bosnian football league to break into three comparatively weak divisions along ethnic lines, with Bosniak, Serb, and Croat teams that rarely played against anyone not of their own allegiance. In 2000 the Croat and Bosniak divisions agreed to interethnic play, joined by the Serb league in 2002. During the Yugoslav era Bosnia and Herzegovina had powerful basketball players, and the sport is still widely popular. However, as with football, ethnic division plagued the sport in the 1990s.

During the period of Yugoslav rule, Bosnian athletes competed in many Olympic Games, and the Winter Games of 1984 were held in Sarajevo. (Sarajevo's ski runs built for the Games were later used as firing ranges for Serb and Yugoslav army artillery during the civil war.) Newly independent Bosnia and Herzegovina formed a national Olympic committee in 1992, which the International Olympic Committee recognized in 1993. The country's first Olympic appearance came in 1992 at Barcelona, Spain. Despite the ongoing war, an interethnic team also participated in the 1994 Winter Games at Lillehammer, Nor. Athletes from the country have continued to participate in subsequent Winter and Summer Games.

Bosnia and Herzegovina features large national parks Sutjeska, Kozara, and Una and nature reserves. Mountains and open spaces offer hiking, skiing, and hunting. Hunting is a popular pastime, and assorted hunting societies include thousands of members.

## Media and publishing

In comparison with news outlets in much of communist eastern Europe, the news media in Yugoslavia were relatively independent, censorship being achieved more through implicit threat than through direct intervention. The warring factions during the 1992–95 war appropriated most media for the distribution of propaganda. Following the war, the Federation of Bosnia and Herzegovina and the Republika Srpska each began operating public radio and television stations. Numerous private stations also exist. Among the many newspapers, magazines, and popular journals circulating in Bosnia and Herzegovina are the Sarajevo dailies Dnevni Avaz and Oslobodjenje and the Banja Luka daily Nezavisne Novine.

# History
## Ancient and medieval periods

When the Romans extended their conquests into the territory of modern Bosnia during the 2nd and 1st centuries bce, the people they encountered there belonged mainly to Illyrian tribes. Most of the area of modern Bosnia was incorporated into the Roman province of Dalmatia. During the 4th and 5th centuries ce, Roman armies suffered heavy defeats in this region at the hands of invading Goths. When the Goths were eventually driven out of the Balkans by the Byzantine emperor Justinian I in the early 6th century, the Bosnian territory became, notionally at least, part of the Byzantine Empire.

Slavs began to settle in this territory during the 6th century. A second wave of Slavs in the 7th century included two powerful tribes, the Croats and the Serbs: Croats probably covered most of central, western, and northern Bosnia, while Serbs extended into the Drina River valley and modern Herzegovina. The terms "Serb" and "Croat" were in this period tribal labels; they were subsequently used to refer to the inhabitants of Serbian or Croatian political entities and only later acquired the connotations of ethnic or national identity in the modern sense.

During the late 8th and early 9th centuries, part of northwestern Bosnia was conquered by Charlemagne's Franks. This area later became part of Croatia under King Tomislav. After Tomislav's death in 928, much of Bosnia was taken over by a Serb princedom that acknowledged the sovereignty of the Byzantine Empire. The first written mention of Bosnia was recorded during this period by the Byzantine emperor Constantine VII Porphyrogenitus, who described "Bosona" as a district in "baptized Serbia." The district he referred to was an area much smaller than modern Bosnia and centred on the Bosna River. Soon after Constantine wrote those words, most of the modern territory of Bosnia reverted to Croatian rule.

During the 11th and 12th centuries, Bosnia experienced rule by Byzantium through Croatian or Serbian intermediaries, incorporation into a Serbian kingdom that had expanded northward from the territory of modern Montenegro and Herzegovina, rule by Hungary, and a brief period of renewed Byzantine rule. After the death of the emperor Manuel I Comnenus in 1180, Byzantine rule fell away, and government by Croatia or Hungary was not restored: a Bosnian territory (excluding much of modern Bosnia and all of Herzegovina) thus became, for the first time, an independent entity.

A Bosnian state of some kind existed during most of the period from 1180 to 1463, despite periodic intrusions from the neighbouring kingdom of Hungary, which maintained a theoretical claim to sovereignty over Bosnia. Bosnia enjoyed periods of power and independence, especially under three prominent rulers: Ban Kulin (ruled c. 1180–1204), Ban Stjepan (Stephen) Kotromanić (ruled 1322–53) of the Kotromanić dynasty, and Stjepan's successor, King Tvrtko I (ruled 1353–91). Under Stjepan Kotromanić, Bosnia expanded southward, incorporating the principality of Hum (modern Herzegovina).

During the reign of Tvrtko I, Bosnia reached farther south and acquired a portion of the Dalmatian coast. For a brief period in the late 14th century, Bosnia was the most powerful state in the western Balkans. This Greater Bosnia of Tvrtko's final decades was an exception, however: for most of the medieval period, Bosnia was mainly a landlocked state, isolated and protected by its impenetrable terrain.

One consequence of this isolation was the development of a distinctive Bosnian church. After the schism of 1054 divided Western

(Latin, or Roman Catholic) and Eastern (Eastern Orthodox) Christianity, most of the Bosnian territory (excluding modern Herzegovina) was Latin, but during the long period of isolation from Rome the Bosnian church fell into its own de facto schism, electing its own leaders from among the heads of the monastic houses.

A combination of poor theological training, lax observances, and Eastern Orthodox practices led to frequent complaints from neighbouring areas, beginning in the 1190s, that the Bosnian church was infected with heresy. In 1203 a papal legate was sent to investigate these charges, and Ban Kulin gathered a special council at Bolino Polje (near modern Zenica), where the church leaders signed a declaration promising to undertake a series of reforms. Most involved correcting lax religious practices; in addition, however, they promised not to shelter heretics in their monasteries.

The extent to which these reforms were observed is very uncertain, since over the following century the church in Bosnia became increasingly isolated. Occasional complaints from the 1280s onward still referred to "heretics" in Bosnia, and, by the time the Roman Catholic Franciscans began to operate there in 1340, the official view from Rome was that the entire Bosnian church had fallen into heresy, from which its members needed to be converted.

Beginning in the mid-19th century, many historians argued that the Bosnian church had adopted the extreme dualist heresy of the Bulgarian Bogomils. Evidence for this view came from the papal denunciations of the Bosnians, which sometimes accused them of Manichaeism, the dualist theology on which Bogomil beliefs were based. In addition, Italian and Dalmatian sources referred to the Bosnians as "Patarins," a term used in Italy for a range of heretics including the Cathari, whose beliefs were linked to Bogomilism.

However, later scholarship suggested that the authors of those denunciations had little or no knowledge of the situation inside Bosnia and that confusion may have been caused by the existence of genuine dualist heretics on the Dalmatian coast. Furthermore, the surviving evidence of the religious practices of the Bosnian church shows that its members accepted many things that Bogomils fiercely rejected, such as the sign of the cross, the Old Testament, the mass, the use of church buildings, and the drinking of wine. The Bosnian church should thus be considered an essentially nonheretical branch of the Roman Catholic Church, based in monastic houses in which some Eastern Orthodox practices also were observed.

During the 14th century the Franciscans established a network of friaries in Bosnia and spent more than a century trying to convert members of the Bosnian church to mainstream Catholicism. In 1459 this campaign received the full support of the Bosnian king, Stjepan Tomaš Ostojić, who summoned the clergy of the Bosnian church and ordered them to convert to Roman Catholicism or leave the kingdom. When most of the clergy converted, the back of the Bosnian church was broken.

The final decades of the medieval Bosnian state were troubled by civil war, Hungarian interference, and the threat of invasion by the Turkish Ottoman Empire. Ottoman armies began raiding Serbia in the 1380s and crossed into Bosnian-ruled Hum (Herzegovina) in 1388. King Tvrtko I sent a large force to fight against them alongside the Serbian army at the Battle of Kosovo Polje in the following year. Tvrtko's successor, Stjepan Ostoja, struggled for possession of the crown against his brother Tvrtko II, who was supported first by the Turks and then by the Hungarians after Ostoja's death.

The nobleman Stefan Vukčić also engaged in tactical alliances against the Bosnian rulers, establishing his own rule over the territory of Hum and giving himself the title herceg (duke), from which the name Herzegovina is derived. Ottoman forces captured an important part of central Bosnia in 1448, centred on the settlement of Vrhbosna, which they developed into the city of Sarajevo. In 1463 they conquered most of the rest of Bosnia proper, although parts of Herzegovina and some northern areas of Bosnia were taken over by Hungary and remained under Hungarian control until the 1520s. Vukčić and his son were gradually forced out of their domains, and the last fortress in Herzegovina fell to the Turks in 1482.

## Ottoman Bosnia

Bosnia was rapidly absorbed into the Ottoman Empire and was divided into military-administrative districts, or sanjaks (from the Turkish sancàk, meaning "banner"). In 1580 a broad area covering modern Bosnia and some surrounding areas of Croatia and Serbia was given the full status of an eyalet, or constituent province of the empire. Bosnia enjoyed this status as a distinct entity throughout the rest of the Ottoman period. The Bosnian eyalet was governed by a vizier and administered through a network of junior pashas and local judges.

Land was distributed according to the Ottoman feudal system, in which the holder of a timar (estate) had to report for military duty, bringing and supporting other soldiers. A wide range of taxes was imposed, including the harač, a graduated poll tax on non-Muslims. Also introduced was the notorious system called devşirme, under which Christian boys aged 10 and above were taken off for training in the imperial administration and the Janissary corps, an elite army division. In all these respects, conditions in Bosnia were similar to those in the other conquered areas of Europe.

In one crucial way, however, Bosnia differed from the other Balkan lands (except, later, Albania): a large part of the native population converted to Islam. This was a gradual development; it took more than a hundred years for Muslims to become an absolute majority. There was no mass conversion at the outset, nor mass immigration of Muslims from Anatolia. The fundamental reason for the growth of such a large Muslim population in Bosnia may lie in the earlier religious history of the Bosnian state.

Whereas neighbouring Serbia had benefited from a strong, territorially organized national church, Bosnia had seen competition in most areas between the Bosnian church and the Roman Catholic Church, both of which operated only out of monastic houses. In Herzegovina a third church, the Serbian Orthodox, had competed. Christianity was thus structurally weaker in Bosnia than in almost any other part of the Balkans. The motives that inclined Bosnians to adopt Islam were partly economic: the prosperous cities of Sarajevo and Mostar were also mainly Muslim, and it was not possible to lead a full civic life there without converting to Islam. Other motives included the privileged legal status enjoyed by Muslims and, possibly, a desire to avoid the poll tax on non-Muslims, though Muslims were subject, unlike Christians, both to the alms tax and to the duties of general military service. But the traditional belief that Bosnian noblemen converted en masse to Islam in order to keep their estates has been largely disproved by modern historians.

Another way in which Bosnia differed from other parts of the Ottoman Balkans is that, for most of the Ottoman period, Bosnia was a frontier province, facing some of the empire's most important enemies Austria, Hungary, and Venice. To fill up depopulated areas of northern and western Bosnia, the Ottomans encouraged the migration of large numbers of hardy settlers with military skills from Serbia and Herzegovina. Some of these settlers were Vlachs, members of a pre-Slav Balkan population that had acquired a Latinate language and specialized in stock breeding, horse raising, long-distance trade, and fighting.

Most were members of the Serbian Orthodox Church. Before the Ottoman conquest, that church had had very few members in the Bosnian lands outside Herzegovina and the eastern strip of the Drina valley. There is no definite evidence of any Orthodox church buildings in central, northern, or western Bosnia before 1463. During the 16th century, however, several Orthodox monasteries were built in those parts of Bosnia, apparently to serve the newly settled Orthodox population there.

Major wars affecting Bosnia took place almost every two generations throughout the Ottoman period. Bosnia was an important recruiting ground for Süleyman I's campaign to conquer Hungary (1520–33). There was fighting on Bosnia's borders during his final Hungarian campaign of 1566. And the large-scale Habsburg-Ottoman conflict of 1593–1606 was sparked by fighting in the Bihać region of northwestern Bosnia.

This war left Bosnia financially drained and militarily exhausted. A Venetian-Ottoman war, beginning in the 1640s and lasting until 1669, involved heavy fighting and destruction in parts of western Bosnia. In the Habsburg-Ottoman war of 1683–99, Austria reconquered Ottoman Hungary and Slavonia, sending a flood of Muslim refugees (mainly converted Slavs) into Bosnia. In 1697 a small Austrian army under Prince Eugene of Savoy marched into the heart of Bosnia, put Sarajevo to the torch, and hurried back to Austrian territory, taking thousands of Roman Catholic Bosnians with it.

In the next major war (1714–18) Austria joined forces with Venice; at the Treaty of Passarowitz (Požarevac, Serb.) in 1718, Venetian-ruled Dalmatia was allowed to extend its territory inland, reaching a line that since then has formed part of the southwestern border of Bosnia. Austria invaded Bosnia again in 1736 but was repelled by local forces; at the subsequent peace settlement (the Treaty of Belgrade, 1739), Austria gave up its claim to the territory south of the Sava River. This settlement formed the basis of the northern border of modern Bosnia. Austria seized more territory after invading Bosnia again in 1788, but it yielded up its gains at the peace settlement in 1791.

The chronic fighting weakened Bosnia. War necessitated increased taxation, causing tax revolts. Forced conscription and frequent plague epidemics led to a relative reduction in the Muslim population, which contributed its manpower to Ottoman campaigns throughout the empire and may have suffered disproportionately from the effects of plague in the cities. In the 18th century there was strong growth in the Christian population; by the end of the century the Muslims were probably no longer in the majority.

The social consequences of war also included a change in the system of land tenure: increasingly, the old feudal timar estates were converted into a type of private estate known as a çiftlik, in response to the imperial treasury's need for cash instead of old-style feudal service. The conditions of work demanded of the peasants on these estates were usually much more severe, and these peasants tended increasingly to be Christians, since Muslim peasants were able to acquire smallholdings in their own right.

Nevertheless, Ottoman Bosnia was not permanently sunk in misery. Descriptions of Sarajevo by visiting travelers portray it as one of the wonders of the Balkans, with fountains, bridges, schools, libraries, and mosques. Fine mosques were also built in towns such as Foča and Banja Luka. (Many of these buildings were systematically demolished by Serb forces in 1992–93.) Numerous works of poetry, philosophy, and theology were written. The cities of Sarajevo and Mostar, where such urban culture flourished, enjoyed a large degree of autonomy under elected officials. After war forced the Bosnian viziers to move out of Sarajevo in the 1690s, they found it almost impossible to return, residing instead in the town of Travnik and exercising only limited power. Real local power passed increasingly into the hands of a type of hereditary official (unique to the Bosnian eyalet) known as a kapetan.

The existence of these powerful local institutions meant that Bosnia was well equipped to resist the reforming measures that the Ottoman sultans began to issue in the early 19th century. When Sultan Mahmud II reformed the military in 1826 and abolished the Janissary corps (which had acquired the status of a privileged social institution), the reform was fiercely resisted by local Janissaries in Bosnia. The Ottoman authorities mounted punitive campaigns against the Janissaries' stronghold, Sarajevo, in 1827 and 1828. In 1831 a charismatic young kapetan called Husein seized power in Bosnia, imprisoning the vizier in Travnik. With an army of 25,000 men, Husein then marched into Kosovo to negotiate with the Ottoman grand vizier, demanding local autonomy for Bosnia and an end to the reform process there.

But the grand vizier stirred up a rivalry between Husein and the leading kapetan of Herzegovina, Ali-aga Rizvanbegović, and in the following year Husein's support melted away when a large Ottoman army entered Bosnia. Rizvanbegović's reward was that Herzegovina was separated from the Bosnian eyalet as a distinct territory under his rule. Further reforms announced by Sultan Abdülmecid I, involving new rights for Christian subjects, a new basis for army conscription, and an end to the much-hated system of tax-farming, were either resisted or ignored by the powerful Bosnian landowners.

During these final decades of Ottoman rule, the rise of Serbia as a quasi-autonomous Christian province, from which Muslims were violently expelled, made Bosnian Muslims feel more isolated and vulnerable. The increasing role of foreign powers (especially Austria and Russia) as "protectors" of the interests of Christians in the Balkans also raised Bosnian suspicions. Bosnian landowners, feeling that they could no longer trust the Ottoman authorities in Constantinople (now Istanbul) to maintain their power, frequently turned to more repressive measures against their Christian subjects.

However, two Bosnian governors succeeded in forcing through some of the sultan's reforms and curbing local resistance. The first of these, Omer-paša Latas, crushed a major rebellion in 1850–51 and revoked the separate status of Herzegovina. The second, Topal Osman-paša, introduced a new method of military conscription in 1865 and a completely new administrative system in 1866, dividing Bosnia into seven sanjaks and establishing a consultative assembly. He also built schools, roads, and a public hospital and allowed the two Christian communities to build new schools and churches of their own. Yet the growing tax demands on Bosnian peasants revived local resistance.

In 1875 a revolt against the state tax collectors began among Christian peasants in the Nevesinje region of Herzegovina. Unrest soon spread to other areas of Bosnia, and repressive force was applied both by the new Bosnian governor and by local landowners using their own irregular troops. The revolt aroused enormous popular sympathy in Serbia, which, along with Montenegro, declared war on the Ottoman

Empire in 1876. Russia came into the war on their behalf in the following year.

After the Serbo-Turkish War ended in 1878, the other great powers of Europe intervened at the Congress of Berlin to counterbalance Russia's new influence in the Balkans. The congress decided that Bosnia and Herzegovina, while remaining notionally under Turkish sovereignty, would be occupied and governed by Austria-Hungary. In 1878 Austro-Hungarian troops took control of Bosnia, overcoming vigorous resistance from local Bosnian forces. They also occupied the neighbouring sanjak of Novi Pazar (now in Serbia), which had been one of the seven Bosnian sanjaks in the late Ottoman period.

## Bosnia and Herzegovina under Austro-Hungarian rule

Bosnia and Herzegovina was declared a "crown land" and was governed by a special joint commission under the Common Ministry of Finance. The Ottoman administrative division was preserved, and Ottoman laws were only gradually replaced or supplemented. This policy of gradualism was the most striking aspect of Austro-Hungarian rule in Bosnia and Herzegovina under Common Finance Minister Benjamin Kállay, a specialist in South Slav history who directed Bosnian policy from 1882 to 1903. Indeed, a common criticism of

Austro-Hungarian rule was that little was done to resolve tensions between landlords and peasants.

In other areas, however, Kállay's rule was extremely active. A public works program was initiated, and by 1907 Bosnia and Herzegovina had a well-developed infrastructure, including an extensive railway and road network. Mines and factories were developed, and agriculture was promoted with model farms and training colleges. Three high schools and nearly 200 primary schools were built, although compulsory education was not introduced until 1909.

While he succeeded in many of these areas of practical improvement, Kállay failed in his central political project: developing a Bosnian national consciousness to insulate the people of Bosnia and Herzegovina from the growing movements of Croatian, Serbian, and Yugoslav ("South Slav") nationalism. Roman Catholic and Orthodox people of Bosnia and Herzegovina had begun by the mid-19th century to identify themselves as "Croats" and "Serbs," respectively. At the same time, Muslim intellectuals were campaigning for greater powers over the Islamic institutions of Bosnia and Herzegovina, thereby becoming quasi-political representatives of a Muslim community with its own distinctive interests. During the first decade of the 20th century, new "national organizations" of Muslims, Serbs, and Croats functioned as embryonic political parties. In response, Kállay's successor, István, Freiherr (baron) Burián, granted a degree of autonomy in religious affairs to both the Muslims and the Serbs of Bosnia and Herzegovina.

In October 1908 nationalist feeling was strongly aroused by the sudden announcement that Bosnia and Herzegovina would be fully annexed by Austria-Hungary. The decision, which caught other great powers by surprise and created a diplomatic crisis lasting many months, was prompted by the revolution of the Young Turks in Constantinople. The Young Turks appeared ready to establish a more democratic regime in the Ottoman Empire, which could then plausibly reclaim Turkish rights over Bosnia and Herzegovina.

Inside Bosnia and Herzegovina, one effect of this change was beneficial: Burián felt able to promote democratic institutions, and a parliament (with limited powers) was introduced there in 1910. But the bitter resentment that the annexation caused among Serb and South Slav nationalists led to the growth of revolutionary groups and secret societies dedicated to the overthrow of Habsburg rule. One of these, Mlada Bosna ("Young Bosnia"), was especially active in Bosnian schools and universities.

Tension was heightened by the First Balkan War of 1912–13, in which Serbia expanded southward, driving Turkish forces out of Kosovo, Novi Pazar, and Macedonia. In May 1913 the military governor of Bosnia and Herzegovina, Gen. Oskar Potiorek, declared a state of emergency, dissolved the parliament, closed down Serb cultural associations, and suspended the civil courts. The following year the heir to the Habsburg throne, Archduke Franz Ferdinand, traveled to Bosnia and Herzegovina to review a military exercise. He was killed in Sarajevo on June 28, 1914, by a young assassin from the Mlada Bosna organization, Gavrilo Princip, who had received some assistance from inside Serbia. Austria-Hungary declared war on Serbia one month later, precipitating World War I.

Bosnia and Herzegovina was under Austro-Hungarian military rule throughout World War I, and repressive measures were applied to those Bosnian Serbs whose loyalty was suspect. At the end of the war, Bosnian politicians from each of the three main communities followed the political leaders of Croatia and Slovenia in throwing off Habsburg rule and joining in the creation of a new South Slav state, the Kingdom of Serbs, Croats, and Slovenes.

# Bosnia and Herzegovina in the Yugoslav kingdom

When the constitution of the Kingdom of Serbs, Croats, and Slovenes was finally settled in June 1921, Bosnia and Herzegovina retained no formal status of its own. However, its outline was preserved on the map, in the form of six oblasti (provinces) corresponding to the sanjaks (excluding that of Novi Pazar) of the late Ottoman period. Serfdom was abolished, but Bosnia and Herzegovina remained relatively undeveloped socially and politically. In 1929 the kingdom was renamed Yugoslavia, and a territorial division introduced under King Alexander I's royal dictatorship divided Bosnia and Herzegovina between four new administrative districts called banovine. Bosnia and Herzegovina thus was wiped off the map. Further adjustments were made in 1939, particularly the creation of an expanded Croatian banovina within Yugoslavia that included portions of Bosnian territory. In 1941, after the Axis invasion of Yugoslavia during World War II, the entire Bosnian territory was absorbed into the puppet state known as the Independent State of Croatia.

The killing that took place in Bosnia and Herzegovina between 1941 and 1945 was terrible in both scale and complexity. The Ustaša, the fascist movement that ruled Croatia during the war, exterminated most of Bosnia and Herzegovina's 14,000 Jews and massacred Serbs on a large scale; tens of thousands of Serbs from Bosnia and Herzegovina died in death camps. Two organized resistance movements emerged: a Serbian royalist force known as the Chetniks, led by Draža Mihailović, and the communist Partisan force (including at first Serbs and then also Croats and Muslims), led by Josip Broz Tito.

The sharply divergent aims of the two movements resulted in a civil war. Royalist forces turned increasingly to German and Italian forces for assistance and committed atrocities against Bosnian Muslims. At the same time, some Bosnian Muslims joined an SS division that operated in northern and eastern Bosnia and Herzegovina for six months during 1944, exacting reprisals against the local Serb population. The Partisans liberated Sarajevo in April 1945 and declared a communist "people's government" for Bosnia and Herzegovina later that month. It is estimated that, when considering only the three largest ethnic groups, 164,000 Serbs, 75,000 Muslims, and 64,000 Croats died in Bosnia and Herzegovina during the war.

## Bosnia and Herzegovina in communist Yugoslavia

In 1946 the People's Republic (from 1963, Socialist Republic) of Bosnia and Herzegovina became one of the constituent republics of the Federal People's (from 1963, Socialist Federal) Republic of Yugoslavia. Life in Bosnia and Herzegovina underwent all the social, economic, and political changes that were imposed on the whole of Yugoslavia by its new communist government, but Bosnia and Herzegovina was particularly affected by the abolition of many traditional Muslim institutions, such as Qur'ānic primary schools, rich charitable foundations, and dervish religious orders.

However, a change of official policy in the 1960s led to the acceptance of "Muslim" as a term denoting a national identity: the phrase "Muslim in the ethnic sense" was used in the 1961 census, and in 1968 the Bosnian Central Committee decreed that "the Muslims are a distinct nation." By 1971 Muslims formed the largest single component of the Bosnian population. During the next 20 years the Serb and Croat populations fell in absolute terms as many Serbs and Croats emigrated. In the 1991 census Muslims made up more than two-fifths of the Bosnian population, while Serbs made up slightly less than one-third and Croats one-sixth. From the mid-1990s the term Bosniak replaced Muslim as the name Bosnian Muslims use for themselves.

In the 1980s the rapid decline of the Yugoslav economy led to widespread public dissatisfaction with the political system. This attitude, together with the manipulation of nationalist feelings by politicians, destabilized Yugoslav politics. Independent political parties appeared by 1989. In early 1990 multiparty elections were held in

Slovenia and Croatia. When elections were held in Bosnia and Herzegovina in December, new parties representing the three national communities gained seats in rough proportion to their populations. A tripartite coalition government was formed, with the Bosniak politician Alija Izetbegović leading a joint presidency. Growing tensions both inside and outside Bosnia and Herzegovina, however, made cooperation with the Serbian Democratic Party, led by Radovan Karadžić, increasingly difficult.

In 1991 several self-styled "Serb Autonomous Regions" were declared in areas of Bosnia and Herzegovina with large Serb populations. Evidence emerged that the Yugoslav People's Army was being used to send secret arms deliveries to the Bosnian Serbs from Belgrade (Serbia). In August the Serbian Democratic Party began boycotting the Bosnian presidency meetings, and in October it removed its deputies from the Bosnian assembly and set up a "Serb National Assembly" in Banja Luka. By then full-scale war had broken out in Croatia, and the breakup of Yugoslavia was under way. Bosnia and Herzegovina's position became highly vulnerable.

The possibility of partitioning Bosnia and Herzegovina had been discussed during talks between the Croatian president, Franjo Tudjman, and the Serbian president, Slobodan Milošević, earlier in the year, and two Croat "communities" in northern and southwestern Bosnia and Herzegovina, similar in some ways to the "Serb Autonomous Regions," were proclaimed in November 1991. When the European Community (EC; later succeeded by the European Union) recognized the independence of Croatia and Slovenia in December, it invited Bosnia and Herzegovina to apply for recognition also. A referendum on independence was held during February 29–March 1, 1992, although Karadžić's party obstructed voting in most Serb-populated areas and almost no Bosnian Serbs voted. Of the nearly two-thirds of the electorate that did cast a vote, almost all voted for independence, which President Izetbegović officially proclaimed on March 3, 1992.

## Independence and war

Attempts by EC negotiators to promote a new division of Bosnia and Herzegovina into ethnic "cantons" during February and March 1992 failed: different versions of these plans were rejected by each of the three main ethnic parties. When Bosnia and Herzegovina's independence was recognized by the United States and the EC on April 7, Bosnian Serb paramilitary forces immediately began firing on Sarajevo, and the artillery bombardment of the city by Bosnian Serb units of the Yugoslav army began soon thereafter. During April many of the towns in eastern Bosnia and Herzegovina with large Bosniak populations, such as Zvornik, Foča, and Višegrad, were attacked by a combination of paramilitary forces and Yugoslav army units. Most of the local Bosniak population was expelled from these areas, the first victims in the country of a process described as ethnic cleansing.

Although Bosniaks were the primary victims and Serbs the primary perpetrators, Croats were also among the victims and perpetrators. Within six weeks a coordinated offensive by the Yugoslav army, paramilitary groups from Serbia, and local Bosnian Serb forces brought roughly two-thirds of Bosnian territory under Serb control. In May the army units and equipment in Bosnia and Herzegovina were placed under the command of a Bosnian Serb general, Ratko Mladić.

From the summer of 1992, the military situation remained fairly static. A hastily assembled Bosnian government army, together with some better-prepared Bosnian Croat forces, held the front lines for the rest of that year, though its power was gradually eroded in parts of eastern Bosnia and Herzegovina. The Bosnian government was weakened militarily by an international arms embargo and by a conflict in 1993–94 with Bosnian Croat forces. But later in 1994 Bosnian Croats and Bosniaks agreed to form a joint federation.

The United Nations (UN) refused to intervene in the Bosnian conflict, but UN Protection Force (UNPROFOR) troops did facilitate the delivery of humanitarian aid. The organization later extended its role to the protection of a number of UN-declared "safe areas." However, the UN failed to protect the safe area of Srebrenica in July 1995, when Bosnian Serb forces perpetrated the massacre of more than 7,000 Bosniak men.

Several peace proposals during the war failed, largely because the Bosnian Serbs who controlled about 70 percent of the land by 1994 refused to concede any territory. In February 1994, in the North Atlantic Treaty Organization's first-ever use of force, NATO fighters shot down four Bosnian Serb aircraft that were violating the UN-imposed no-fly zone over the country. Later that year, at the UN's request, NATO launched isolated and ineffective air strikes against Bosnian Serb targets. But following the Srebrenica massacre and another Bosnian Serb attack on a Sarajevo marketplace, NATO undertook more concentrated air strikes late in 1995.

Combined with a large-scale Bosniak-Croat land offensive, this action led Bosnian Serb forces to agree to U.S.-sponsored peace talks in Dayton, Ohio, U.S., in November. Serbian Pres. Slobodan Milošević represented the Bosnian Serbs. The resulting Dayton Accords called for a federalized Bosnia and Herzegovina in which 51 percent of the land would constitute a Croat-Bosniak federation and 49 percent a Serb republic. To enforce the agreement, formally signed in December 1995, a 60,000-member international force was deployed.

It was originally estimated that at least 200,000 people were killed and more than 2,000,000 displaced during the 1992–95 war. Subsequent studies, however, concluded that the death toll was actually about 100,000.

## Postwar Bosnia and Herzegovina

An election in September 1996 produced a tripartite national presidency chaired by Izetbegović and an ethnically apportioned national legislature dominated by nationalist parties. Karadžić had been indicted for war crimes and was prohibited from being a candidate, though he retained some support among Bosnian Serbs into the 21st century. (He eluded capture until his arrest in Belgrade in July 2008.) The national government was largely responsible for foreign affairs, and the internationally appointed Office of the High Representative established under the Dayton Accords and later granted overriding executive powers (the so-called Bonn Powers) oversaw the implementation of the peace agreement and acted as the final authority. Meanwhile, the two parts of the republic, the Bosniak-

Croat Federation of Bosnia and Herzegovina and the Republika Srpska (Bosnian Serb Republic), were largely autonomous, each having its own assembly.

Over the next several years the country experienced an uneasy peace. It received extensive international assistance, but the economy remained in shambles. Much of the workforce was unemployed about 50 percent in the Federation and about 70 percent in the Republika Srpska. By the early 21st century, however, projects funded by the World Bank had succeeded in reconstructing much of the country's infrastructure, and some political and economic reforms were implemented.

In the course of the regional economic boom of 2006–08, unemployment in the country fell to less than 30 percent. As European bank credit and foreign direct investment took the place of declining international aid, rates of economic growth averaged 6 percent. Although the international financial crisis that began in 2008 did affect the economy, it had less of an impact in Bosnia and Herzegovina than elsewhere in the Balkans, as the country's current account and state budget deficits were relatively small. Regional relations also improved in the early 21st century. In both the Croat and Serb communities, calls for breaking away from Bosnia and Herzegovina to unite with

Croatia and Serbia declined in the face of faded interest from both of those states. Relations with Croatia in particular warmed in 2010, following Croatian Pres. Ivo Josipović's apology for his country's military actions in Bosnia and Herzegovina during the warfare of the early 1990s.

Nonetheless, other problems have continued to delay the internal integration of Bosnia and Herzegovina, leaving in doubt the possibility of accession into the European Union (EU). Although the danger of renewed violence has remained minimal, the stalemate between the Federation and the Republika Srpska has persisted. Struggles over a potential new constitution, including disputed provisions for a common police force, have steadfastly resisted resolution. The international Office of the High Representative has remained in place, despite repeated attempts to end its authority and transfer its advisory functions to an EU office.

Underlying all these difficulties are the continuing troubled relations between Bosniaks and Bosnian Serbs. Their leaders' respective demands for a federation with some central powers in Sarajevo and a loose confederation offering the right of secession have been diametrically opposed. Their disagreement has frustrated repeated efforts to draft a new constitution to replace the Dayton agreement.

Some promise for progress did emerge from the elections of October 2010. Although the hard-line president of the Republika Srpska, Milorad Dodik, was reelected, the Bosniak presidency passed to Bakir Izetbegović, the son of Bosnia and Herzegovina's first president, Alija Izetbegović. Attracting younger voters to his campaign for reconciliation, he joined Bosnian Croat Pres. Željko Komšić as a moderating figure.

In May 2011 Ratko Mladić, who had commanded the Bosnian Serb forces during the war and was widely held to be responsible for the Srebrenica massacre, was captured in Serbia to be extradited to The Hague for trial on charges of genocide and crimes against humanity.

The political deadlock that had hobbled the Bosnian government since the October 2010 election was finally resolved on December 28, 2011. The absence of a central government had threatened to spark a financial crisis, as foreign investment contracted and hundreds of millions of dollars from the EU and the International Monetary Fund were withheld. The six major political parties agreed on Bosnian Croat Vjekoslav Bevanda as a compromise choice as prime minister, and they began work on a budget that would allow the new government to function.

## Urbanism, Architecture, and the Use of Space

Approximately 42 percent of the population lives in towns or cities. Sarajevo, near the center of the country in a valley of the Dinaric Alps, is the capital and largest city. Once a cultural center and tourist destination (it was the site of the 1984 Winter Olympics), it has been devastated by the civil war. Before the war, it was a vibrant, cosmopolitan mixture of the old and the new, with skyscrapers and modern buildings standing alongside ancient Turkish mosques and marketplaces. Today many of these buildings are in rubble, and food and electricity are in short supply. Despite its desperate situation, Sarajevo has taken in many refugees from other parts of the country. Even amid the destruction, however, there is evidence of Sarajevo's glorious past. The Turkish Quarter boasts the Gazi

Husrev-Bey mosque, which dates back to the sixteenth century. The religious architecture is varied and impressive; in addition to mosques, there are several Orthodox churches, a cathedral, and a Sephardic Jewish synagogue. The city also has a history museum and a national art gallery.

Mostar, the largest city in the Herzegovina region, also has been devastated by the civil war. Other major cities include Banja Luka,

Zenica, and Tuzla. Before the war, housing in the cities consisted primarily of concrete apartment buildings. Many of those structures were destroyed during the war, and despite efforts at rebuilding, many remain unlivable. People have been forced into crowded living situations with little privacy.

In rural areas, which are much less densely populated, the effects of war have been less extreme. Most of those houses are small structures of stone or wood. Before the war, the majority of them were equipped with electricity and running water.

Samuel Matthews

# Travel and Tourism

Often described as a crossroad of civilizations, Bosnia and Herzegovina is a mountainous playground that is quickly becoming a popular tourist destination. This long forgotten jewel of southern Europe is now third in the world in terms of tourism growth rate, and it is easy to see why. The stunning landscapes combined with historical and cultural heritage make it one of the most fascinating countries to visit in Europe. Curiosity attracts first-timers, but it is the never-ending natural wonders that lure travelers back again and again. The westernmost point of the East and easternmost point of the West, Bosnia and Herzegovina is a must-see, especially for active vacationers.

The great outdoors is often the central theme of tour packages to Bosnia and Herzegovina. Its architecture is also a major draw. In the capital of Sarajevo, you will find cobblestone streets lined by an intriguing mix of religious edifices and lively cafés. Away from the city are many other delights, such as the medieval town of Jajce, its citadel along and the Old Bridge of Mostar. Adventure-seekers will not run out of things to do in the unspoiled Sutjeska National Park.

Bosnia and Herzegovina is a real treat for hikers and cyclers. The country hosted the Winter Olympics in 1984, proof that its mountains have great potential for winter sports. Avid skiers flock to the slopes of the Bjelasnica and Igman Mountains. Water adventures are also popular, with majestic rivers criss-crossing scenic destinations throughout the country.

Having successfully emerged from wars and territorial disputes, Bosnia and Herzegovina is now a safe place to visit. Memories of unrest have been laid to bed in the history books, museums and monuments. The country's Turkish heritage is still very much alive in the capital, evident in stunning Ottoman mosques and monasteries that stand side by side Catholic shrines, Orthodox churches, and temples, showing peace despite cultural diversity. Archaeological excavations throughout the country reveal tribal life that can be traced back 12,000 years.

Bosnians and Herzegovinians are welcoming and hospitable. In fact, it is not rare for complete strangers to invite guests for a cup of coffee in one of the trendy cafés of Sarajevo. The capital offers many choices of accommodation from basic apartments to luxurious five-star hotels that rival the best in the world. Outside the city, independent hotels, bed and breakfasts popular with couples, and motels are common. Backpackers can rest their feet at private houses marked *zimmer* or *sobe*, indicating they have rooms for rent.

It is possible to reach Bosnia and Herzegovina by plane, train, or even international bus, all of which converge in the capital. Sarajevo Airport in the Butmir suburb is the main gateway into the country, with flights to and from major European cities. Trains connect to Hungary, Serbia, and Croatia, but services are infrequent. International buses are a better option, with regular trips to and from neighboring countries. Ferry services connect to key cities on the Adriatic, while inter-city boats ply inland lakes and rivers. Trains are intermittent, even within the country, so it is advisable to take a bus or rent a car when getting between places.

## Things to Do

Some of the wonders of Bosnia and Herzegovina have been fractured and damaged by conflict, but the surviving attractions will make you forget a war ever happened. The lively urban hubs have plenty to offer the cosmopolitan traveler. Sarajevo's Bascarsija district, for example, is best known for its Turkish cafés and trinket shops. History buffs will enjoy the emblematic Ottoman bridge, which best symbolizes the rise of a new Bosnia and Herzegovina.

Beyond the towering minarets and mosques, cobblestone streets and city life of Sarajevo are opportunities for expeditions around the most beautiful mountain and river destinations in the country. Outdoor enthusiasts will find plenty of things to do between rafting, kayaking, fly fishing and canyoning tours. The mountains of Bjelasnica, Jahorina, and Igman are littered with ski resorts and challenging trails, not only for winter explorations, but for summer treks, as well.

The Neretva River is the most popular place for water sports in Bosnia and Herzegovina and offers all kinds of extreme adventures, most notably rafting. Equally beautiful river areas like the Drina, Una and Tara are also worth a trip. Whitewater rafting is best on the Krivaja River, while shorter courses can be found on the Sana and Vrbas rivers. *Una Regatta Sport Bijeli* is the guide to turn to for packages, whether you are traveling with friends, family or getting wet and wild on your own.

With turquoise rivers cutting through dramatic, rocky mountains that carpet most of the country, Bosnia and Herzegovina features finest outdoor pursuits Balkan peninsula has to offer. There are very few tourists who visit Bosnia each year, keeping the experience sweet and authentic for those who choose the path less taken. Hiking trails, gorges, and mountain villages are packed with opportunities for adventure and discovery.

I spend 10 amazing days in Bosnia, starting from Sarajevo, all the way to the southernmost town of Trebinje. My trip was filled with adrenaline and stunning views as I spent most of my days up in the mountains. One morning, I was awoken by a flock of sheep passing by under my window. It could have been nearly a hundred of them! Nowadays it isn't easy to find such unspoiled places in Europe. Untouched, pristine nature is only one of the reason why you should visit Bosnia.

People sometimes tend to associate Bosnia and Herzegovina with war and think of the place as it was back in the 1990s, but a lot has changed over the past two decades. I found the country easy to travel through, with the local people being warm, friendly and incredibly welcoming

**Canyoning** is another popular way to satisfy your craving for adrenaline. Rakitnica Canyon has excellent routes and the most extreme courses can be found around the beautiful Bjela River. *Scorpio Outdoors and Adventure Agency* offers year-round canyoning tours along with other adventure persuits like rock climbing, skiing, hiking, and mountain biking.

Bosnia and Herzegovina is a popular eco-tourism destination that can be explored by small group bus trips through *Balkan Road Trip*. Fishing tours are also available and are especially popular with fly fishing enthusiasts. *Plaza Dzajica buk* specializes in water-based recreation including whitewater rafting and hunting.

Winter sports are easy to find in the mountainous Bosnia and Herzegovina. In fact, skiing is one of the most popular activities. Bijelasnica and Viscocica mountains have exceptional resorts and facilities, along with beautiful mountain towns around Sarajevo. *Scorpio* offers active ski adventures and mountain packages.

**Hiking** trails around the country rival those around the world. Bosnia and Herzegovina's mountain regions are known for their rugged and stunning scenery. Be sure to visit the sprawling Sutjeska National Park where *Mountain Travel Sobek* offers treks.

**City tours** are also worthwhile, whether you want a pilgrimage or simple sightseeing to some of the most historic spots in the country. The capital is a good base and *Sarajevo Discovery* offers plenty of options.

# Other things to do
## Hidden-Bosnia and Herzegovina
## Zeljava Airbase
Yugoslavia's biggest underground airport lies in ruins.
*In the movie Star Wars: The Empire Strikes Back, the rebels keep their spacecraft hidden in an underground base, to come out only when striking at the Empire. Željava Air Base was Communist Yugoslavia's version of that base.*

Situated in the west of Bosnia on the border with Croatia, Objekat 505, as it was officially known, was the largest underground airport in the Balkans. The primary purpose of the Objekat 505 was to house a long-range radar early warning system, akin to NORAD, as well as to provide a strategic command center for the country's defense.

The construction of the base was conducted in utmost secrecy between 1957 and 1965, and the cost of its construction was a whopping six billion dollars, three times more than the combined yearly military budgets of Yugoslavia's two biggest successor states, Serbia and Croatia. The secret airbase was positioned at the center of a dense sprawling network of military installations, with five auxiliary airfields nearby as well as numerous radar and air defense outposts.

The resulting base was a military marvel, an underground airport with four exits, each of which was capable of launching jets. The base housed two full hunter squadrons. The base was designed to sustain a direct hit by a 20-kiloton nuclear warhead, the equivalent of the Nagasaki bomb, and it could be hermetically sealed. The base could also house up to 1,000 people and stored provisions for up to 30 days. Objekat 505 also had access to an underground water supply and a power generator. Fuel for the generator was brought into the base by deep pipes coming from an underground storage facility near the town of Bihać.

The base was intended to protect the country from the foreign aggression. Unfortunately, its designers had not taken into account the possibility of a civil war. On October 25, 1991, on the eve of the war, Rudolf Perešin, one of the fighter pilots stationed in the base, an ethnic Croat who did not want to fight, defected and escaped the base via the fourth exit. He was also not the only one; not too long afterwards, Daniel Borović also defected with his jet, though he managed to land at Zagreb Airport (Perešin had to divert to Klagenfurt in Austria, his jet now on display at Zeltweg Airbase). Even though they did not depart from the base itself, two other pilots - Ivan Selak and Ivica Ivandić - were also based there, but transferred to Užice in Serbia following Željava's destruction.

During its retreat from this region of Bosnia, the Yugoslav National Army decided to destroy the functionality of the airbase to avoid its use by any of the factions in the conflict. They did so by setting off built-in explosive charges. A year later, the demolition of the base was completed by the military of the then Republic of Serbian Krajina, and an additional 56 tons of explosive were detonated. The explosion was so powerful that it was felt in all the way in Bihać.

Today the abandoned airbase lies on the border of Croatia and the Bosnian Federation, with the line dividing the countries running through the middle of the property. Extreme caution needs to be used when approaching this site, due to the large number of unexploded landmines and other munitions there. The police force of the Bosnian Federation uses the area of the airbase to train its K9 core in explosive retrieval.

## Watermills of Jajce

This cluster of little wooden huts once ground local farmers' wheat into flour during the days of the Austro-Hungarian Empire

*Jajce, in the central region of Bosnia and Herzegovina, is a historic city all about falling water. Famous for its enormous waterfall in the middle of town, the meeting of two rivers – the Pliva and the Vrbas – established the region in the 14th century as the capital of the then*

*Kingdom of Bosnia. There's a town castle, old fortified city walls, high mountains and deep river valleys. And just downstream, in the area of the Pliva Lakes, is a collection of about 20 little huts that once served as watermills for local farmers*

The little windowless huts sit on top of skinny stilts right over the gushing water. Since the flow here is spread out, by using a series of little mills instead of one big water wheel, the diffuse water power could be aggregated. Pretty ingenious. Most of the huts go back to the period of the Austro-Hungarian empire (about 1867 to 1918), and they give the impression of a little storybook village.

No longer used for actual milling, the Pliva Lakes watermills draw tourists down the river from the giant waterfall in town. That one is certainly impressive with its showy 65-foot drop. But the little shingled watermills feel like they might be home to some local trolls, with their dragons hitched up out back.

## Tjentiste War Memorial

These warring psychedelic crags commemorate an unsuccessful military operation.
*One of the many otherworldly monuments that dot the Bosnian landscape, the rocky passage of the Tjentiste War Memorial is a stunning tribute to a total failure.*

The two fractal walls of the memorial were erected in the 1970's to remember *Operation Fall Schwarz,* otherwise known as the Battle of the Sutjeska. The military action took place during World War II and saw Axis forces attempt to rout a group of Yugoslavian forces and capture their leader. The complicated battle saw most of the Yugoslav forces able to escape, including their leader, foiling the Nazis' plan, which was actually the second attempt at the same strategy. While the the Axis' plan was a failure, it was not without tragedy. Over 7,000 people were killed, mostly just citizens who could not escape with the majority of the Yugoslavian military forces.

To remember both the Nazi failure and the tragic loss of life, the abstract war memorial was constructed. Like many of the memorials constructed in Bosnia and Herzegovina during the 70's the monument is an angular abstraction constructed from bleak grey cement. However despite the tragic roots and brutalist construction, the majestic strangeness of the Tjentiste

## Stari Most
Bridge that died in war and was resurrected.
*The Bosnian War of the early 1990s had many victims, both human and architectural. One of the best known among these was the Old Bridge of Mostar. Once one of the most iconic landmarks of Bosnia and*

*the old Yugoslav federation, the bridge was destroyed by Croatian armed forces on November 9, 1993. It is unclear why the Croatian army would have destroyed such a historic bridge, except as an act of vengeance (of which there were many on all sides of the conflict), as the bridge had no military significance*

The bridge, a masterpiece of Ottoman Turkish architecture, was commissioned by none other then Suleiman the Magnificent, and designed by Mimar Hayruddin, a student of the famous Mimar Sinan. The construction began in 1557 and took nine years to complete. Elegant in its simplicity, the bridge consists of a single 30-meter-wide and 24-meter-high arc, connecting the steep riverbanks of Neretva river. Two towers protect the entrances to the bridge. These massive stone structures stand in sharp contrast to the streamlined silhouette of the bridge, only emphasizing its beauty.

The surrounding city of Mostar even owes its name to the bridge, "most" meaning bridge in Serbo-Croatian.

After the end of the Bosnian War, the bridge was reconstructed from 2001 to 2004. Much of original stone were salvaged from the bottom of the river. The rest was replaced with new blocks quarried from the same locations used for the original construction. A coalition of international organizations led by the World Bank and UNESCO financed the reconstruction.

Diving into river from the highest point of the bridge has been a test of courage for local young men for as long as anyone can remember. Tourists can pay locals to make the dive for their viewing pleasure. Official annual bridge-jumping competitions started in 1968 and are still held each summer. In 2015, the Red Bull Cliff Diving World Series was held in Mostar.

## Kravice Waterfalls

There's a mini version of Iguazu Falls hidden in the Balkans... and it's got a rope swing.

*Situated on the Trebižat River amidst Europe's last jungle lies a series of waterfalls that conjure images more in keeping with the Swiss Family Robinson than those traditionally Balkan.*

Plunging from cliffs as high as 83 feet into a natural, watery amphitheater that is almost 500 feet across, the series of waterfalls at Kravice are nestled in a natural reserve southwest of the city of Mostar in Bosnia and Herzegovina. The collective impression created is one of a more approachable, kid sister to the thunderous Iguazu Falls spanning Brazil and Argentina's border that remains less visited, and unspoiled in a way its big brother can no longer claim.

The rapids at the base of the falls aren't particularly dangerous even in the springtime, and no lifeguards are charged with policing activities. This makes the natural swimming holes at Kravice local favorites despite the water's year-round chilly temperature. As if bathing beneath cascading waters and leaping from rock to rock weren't enough, a rope swing has even been added for bonus kicks. With a bar on its banks, a classic mill and old sailing ship moored in the lake at its base, Kravice Falls leaves nothing wanting.

Tour groups can be hired to bring you to Kravice, but part of the joy in experiencing Kravice Falls is its general lack of crowds, which means joining a large cluster of strangers bound for the falls may just defeat the purpose of the place. Knowledgable visitors instead recommend renting a car from Mostar or negotiating taxi service to and from the woods, the latter of which merely adds to the adventure by tossing in the fun of haggling over price.

## Sarajevo Bobsleigh Track

A war-torn Olympic relic is being overtaken by graffiti and nature
*Once a proud feature of Sarajevo's 1984 Winter Olympic games, the bobsleigh track has since fallen into ruin after being the victim of military actions*

The 1300-meter concrete track was completed in 1982 and featured a total of 13 turns for the lugers to navigate. The expensive public work paid off for the country after the events around the site during the Olympics garnered enormous crowds. The track was able to be reused during World Cup competitions in later years following the winter games and it appeared that the long track would continue to pay dividends. Unfortunately when the Yugoslav Wars began in 1991, the track, like the rest of the country, became embroiled in the fighting. The curled turns were used as defensive positions for Bosnian forces, and the whole of the track became pocked with bullet holes and other wounds.

Today, the track still stands as a favorite spot for local graffiti artists who have decorated whole swaths of the curving lane. The Sarajevo Bobsleigh Track is a literally concrete reminder of a more prosperous time. It is currently under re-construction for future bobsleigh competitions but official guided tours are still available.

**Know Before You Go**
Do not wander around this area alone or without a local who knows it perfectly; there are still many unexploded mines littering the hillside. Venturing off the established paths is not advised. However, many travelers do hike this medium-difficult trek through the houses on Mount Trebević. Alternatively, there are tours which cater for those

who do not want to hike or local buses which go three-quarters of the way there. You can also hire a taxi and your driver may act as your tour guide for the trip, just be patient and negotiate the price before getting in.

## Sarajevo War Tunnel Museum

**This museum preserves the hand-dug tunnel that kept Sarajevo afloat during the Serbian siege.**

*During a large portion of the 1990s Sarajevo was under siege by Serbian forces who controlled almost the entire city. However, Bosniak loyalists built a tunnel which would secretly supply much of the rest of the city during the occupation.*

Begun in January of 1993 under the codename "Objekt BD," the tunnel was built to link the Bosnian neighborhoods of Butmir and Dobrinja under a Serbian-controlled aircraft runway. The crude tunnel was dug by hand and shovel from both sides, by workers who chiseled away at the earth in eight-hour shifts. The clandestine laborers, who were paid in cigarettes, had to contend with near constant shelling and underground water which would rise to waist high in the cramped tunnel and had to be emptied one bucket at a time. The two tunnels finally met in July of 1993 creating an 800-meter lifeline between the two neighborhoods. Once completed the tunnel had an average height of one and half meters, and was shored up with tons of steel and concrete. A small railway was finally built into the floor and crucial food, gas, and weapons were finally able to be secreted into the very heart of the siege.

After the war ended the tunnel was abandoned, but a museum was built in the building which covered the Dobrinja entrance. The museum displays weaponry and ephemera from the war and allows visitors to explore a short distance into the tunnel. The war may be over, but the Sarajevo War Tunnel Museum makes sure that no one will forget the unstoppable determination and resourcefulness of Sarajevo's citizens.

## Čolina Kapa Astronomical Observatory

The haunting ruins of a military fortress turned astronomical observatory sit on a Sarajevo mountaintop.
*During World War II, an Austro-Hungarian military fortress was built on Mount Trebević. The mountaintop provided views of the entire city, and was a key point in military observation. After the war this lookout point proved useful again, when the fortress was converted into an astronomical observatory.*

The Orion Astronomical Society established the Čolina Kapa Observatory and worked hard to bring it up to state-of-the-art technological standards. By 1972, it was the only facility of its kind in Bosnia and Herzegovina. Its three domes crowned the building waiting for astronomers to observe the night sky, while the fortress below contained all that visiting scholars might need for several days' stay, including a reference library and a photo lab. Research done at the observatory led to the publishing of a photographic atlas of the North sky compiled from the images taken here.

Unfortunately, two decades later in the 1990s much of Sarajevo was devastated by shelling during the Bosnian War. The astronomical observatory was no exception. The Čolina Kapa Observatory and all its instruments were completely destroyed between 1992 and 1995. The area was absolutely shattered by the conflict, and without adequate funding, the observatory was abandoned.

Today it remains an important symbol of Sarajevo, as its white building still looks over the city from Mount Trebević, though today the walls are crumbling and decrepit. Though the abandoned building is a popular attraction for urban exploring hikers, most Sarajevans would prefer that the observatory be restored.

Without Čolina Kapa, astronomy is virtually non-existant in Bosnia and Herzegovina, despite the fact that the study of the stars reaches back to the 15th century in the region. A fundraising campaign has been launched with the intention of "bringing astronomy back to Sarajevo.

## Canyoning

If you love the adrenaline, accept the challenge of Bosnia's longest and deepest canyon. A tour through Rakitnica canyon takes 8 hours of climbing, hiking and sliding through water. This was really one of the highlights of my trip, although I certainly reached my own physical limits. This canyon is really spectacular!

It was the first time I used the hydrospeed – a water sled that supports one's body. It saved my life as it helped me avoid crashing into major stone formations (some at least:-) ). The water pressure in Rakytnica is quite high, with many rapids and waterfalls.

This tour organised by Visit Konjic costs EUR 75 per person. Equipment, lunch package and transportation. Ask for Armin, he is really experienced.

## Rafting

Mastering the wild river in a large rubber boast is probably the most popular outdoor activity and a must-do in Bosnia. Tara river should be the most challenging. I did the calmer Neretva and really loved it. The river is emerald-green and carves through a deep rock valley. What a scenery!

The rafting trip takes the whole day (from 10am to 7pm), but it is more relaxed than canyoneering. There were some rapids on the way, the rest was just about paddling and enjoying the landscape. And, the lunch was a delicious BBQ on the bank of the river.

Thanks to Aldin and Anel from Visit Konjic for being great guides and keeping us safe. The tour costs EUR 50 per person.

## Hiking

The unspoiled nature and the picturesque mountains were the real highlight of my travel to Bosnia. Speaking for myself, I loved Bjelasnica mountains the best, but there are a lot of hiking possibilities. This country is really perfect destination for hiking!

### Hike from Umoljani to Lukomir village

My first and favourite hike. The starting point is in Umoljani, about one hour drive from Sarajevo, at about 1900 meters above sea level. After mastering several mountains and valleys (the views are just stunning), we finished the tour in Lukomir, the highest mountain settlement in Bosnia at 1,469m. There were really lots of sheep on this

trip

**Practical info**: 4 hours hike, 8 kilometres hiking distance. I did it with Superb Adventures, the trip cost EUR 50 including an overnight stay in Lukomir and two meals. Thanks to our entertaining guide Faruk

### Hike to Hajdučka vrata arch

This hiking trail is located on Mt Čvrsnica, known as a popular skiing spot during the winter. The hiking trail starts at 1458 meters above sea level, going up at a moderate steep to 2003 metres. At the end, there is the spectacular Hajdučka vrata, a more than four meters wide natural stone arch formed by carts and limestone. From there we returned the same way, but there are other options as well.

**Practical info**: This is a 9 kilometres hike. If you are interested in this trip, Visit Konjic has several options for this tour. The highest mountain house in Bosnia is also near there.

### Along the border with Montenegro

Southern Herzegovina has some great hiking, too. You can pair this trip with visiting the charming town of Trebinje. It's an easy six kilometres hike connecting several old Austro-Hungarian military spots and graves of Austrian soldiers. Advanced hikers can climb Jastrebica peak at 1864 meters. The fun part is that you are actually at the Montenegro border, so you might just cross it and come back. Don't forget your passport:-)

**Practical info**: The hike to Jastrebica takes 3,5 hours. When arranging tours around Trebinje, contact Sinisa from Walk with me. He can guide you from EUR 10-20.

## Mountain biking

Mountain biking is another cool thing to do in Bosnia. It's a great way to have fun and do something for your health as well. No matter if you choose the easy or difficult one, I can only give you one piece of advice – take care and don't use your breaks on the stones. Because well, I did – and I can tell you that falling down wasn't so great (mountain bikes seem to be my enemy, I already fell in Austria). Luckily, my experienced guide rescued me and then I could continue the trip!

We cycled from Ruište-Boračko lake onwards, only part of the trail that normally leads to Konjic, 40 kilometers in total.

**Practical info**: This trip with Visit Konjic costs EUR 60 including the bike renta

# Travel to Bosnia and Herzegovina

The most convenient way to travel to Bosnia is by airplane. There are low cost flights landing in Tuzla International Airport (from Netherlands, Germany and Scandinavia), but it is a bit off the map.

Landing in Sarajevo airport can safe you plenty of time. Find best price with Kiwi.com.

If you are going to visit Bosnia from other European destination, you can do it overland as well. There are two daily trains running from Sarajevo to Zagreb (10 hours) as well as various long distance buses: to Belgrade, Kotor, Ljubjana and several other cities in Croatia (Zagreb, Split, Rijeka, Pula and Dubrovnik).

Bosnia offers nearly endless opportunities for adventure travellers, longing to experience nature and the wild outdoors. During my trip, I got to experience some of the most adrenaline filled tours.

## Attractions

It's hard to sum up the beauty of Bosnia and Herzegovina on a straight list of attractions. In Sarajevo alone, you'll find countless historic buildings, all perfectly blending with the cosmopolitan and commercial vibe of the new city. Bordered by Serbia, Montenegro, Croatia, and Dalmatia, Bosnia and Herzegovina also dips a toe in the Adriatic, giving way to the only beach in the country. If there's one thing that keeps visitors hooked, it's the gorgeous mountain ranges, providing all kinds of adventures and nature trips with breathtaking cliffs, trails, rivers, and challenging slopes. Best of all, the mountain towns in Bosnia and

Herzegovina are relatively close to the cosmopolitan center so you won't be wasting valuable time traveling.

**Bascarsija, Sarajevo:** The Bascarsija district in Sarajevo is more than just a centuries-old market. This old part of the town dates back to the 15th century and highlights cultural diversity. A physical display of the struggle to absorb strong religious influences into an already diverse territory, very few places in the world are like Sarajevo where mosques, Catholic and Orthodox churches, synagogues, and temples all stand harmoniously within walking distance of each other. Address: Sarajevo, Bosnia and Herzegovina

**Stari Most:** Mostar's old bridge is one of the finest examples of Ottoman architecture in Bosnia and Herzegovina. It is also one of the most photographed sites, especially with its stunning river, mountain, and city backdrop. This iconic symbol represents a meeting point between eastern and western civilizations. The precious stone structure has been rebuilt and restored to its former glory after a heartbreaking collapse due to tank shelling in the early 1990's. Address: Neretva River, Mostar

**Sutjeska National Park:** Historically a WWII battlefield as evidenced by imposing stone monuments that commemorate Partisan victory over German armies, Sutjeska National Park is also home to one of the last two remaining primeval forests in Europe, known as the Perucica Forest. Its 17,500 hectares of wilderness are home to all kinds of natural wonders, including the country's highest peak, Maglic Mountain, along with the picture-perfect Skakavac Waterfall. The ancient forest, riverside, and mountains all provide great hiking trails, some more challenging than others. Address: Sarajevo Region, Bosnia and Herzegovina

**Jahorina Mountain:** Since the 1984 Bosnian Olympics, the slopes of Jahorina have become the go-to place for winter sports. The mountain range is just a few miles southeast of the capital, with its highest peak at 6,266 feet. Ski lifts guarantee fabulous views of the city below and the downhill descent will give you a quick rush of adrenaline.Address: Jahorina Mountain, Sarajevo Region Phone: +387-65-414-413 (Winter Center Jahorina) Website:http://www.jahorina.org/en/ (Winter Center Jahorina)

**Travnik:** Nestled in the Lasva River valley, Travnik is one of the most attractive historic towns in the country. Its ancient mosque and old fortress dominate the skyline and it is a popular starting point for visits to the nearby mountain resort of Vlasic. The town is home to centuries-old mansions and castles, all well preserved since Roman times and the Ottoman empire. Address: Central Bosnia

**Kraljeva Sutjeska:** Known as one of the last seats of the medieval Bosnian Kingdom, this ancient museum will take you on an instant time warp, with its white stone houses, monastery and oversized Franciscan church. The Dusper House is especially striking despite its dilapidated state, while the old mosque greets visitors right at the entrance to the village. Address: Sarajevo Region, Bosnia and Herzegovina

**Bosnian Kingdom Trail:** The Bosnian Kingdom Trail consists of several ancient towns. The Visoko Valley, for example, once served as an important cultural, trade, and educational center, while the towns of Vranduk in Zenica, Bobovac, Kraljeva Sutjeska, Maglaj, Tesnaj, Fojnica, Travnik, Prusac, and Jajce are all home to a wide range of interesting remnants of the Bosnian Kingdom. Address: Bosnia and Herzegovina Phone: +387-32-733-186 (Tourist Information Centre, Visoko)

**Medjugorje:** Medjugorje is the site of the apparition Mary, mother of Jesus Christ. It sits on a barren hillside between Bijakovici and Medugorje villages, and is the place of one of the world's largest Catholic pilgrimages. The story of the six teenagers who witnessed the ghost while playing on the hills is widely known to Catholics and millions of faithful patrons visit the sacred spot every year. Address: Herzegovina Region

**Neum:** On the Adriatic Sea, Neum is Bosnia's only beach. It attracts thousands of visitors every year who long for sun and sea. The coast is a great starting-off point for all kinds of aquatic pursuits, from scuba diving to parasailing, jet-skiing, and even boat tours. The small strip is lined by hundreds of hotels, guesthouses and many other types of private accommodation. Address: Herzegovina Region

## Food and Restaurants

Bosnian and Herzegovinians have a meat-centric diet. Traditional cuisine has obvious Turkish influences, and there is no shortage of the ubiquitous Balkan kebab. There are restaurants just about everywhere, even in small towns, where flame grilled meat and meat stews are staples. Don't miss the succulent *jagnjetina*, grilled mutton or lamb, as well as *bosanski ionac*, a form of meat stew that is cooked on an open fire. Many good restaurants are sprinkled around Sarajevo's central shopping district, as well as in the old town and they all serve exquisite and reasonably priced food.

### Bars and Pubbing in Bosnia and Herzegovina

Nightlife is vibrant everywhere in Bosnia and Herzegovina, especially in the capital. Clubs and bars stay open until early morning, but if you prefer people-watching, trendy cafés can be found along major attractions. *Opera Bar* (B Sarajeva 25, Sarajevo) is a popular stop for opera-goers and people in the performance arts community. It's also an excellent place for espresso and traditional Turkish coffee. *Connectum/Klub Knjige*(Veliki Curciluk 27, Sarajevo) is worth a visit for a typical bookstore-café experience.

If it's lively beats and electric crowds you are looking for, head to Sarajevo's nightclubs and cocktail bars. Thursdays, Fridays, and Saturdays are the busiest, so think about reserving a table or at least arriving early to secure a spot in popular places like *Central Café* (Strosmajerova 1, Bascarsija), known for its tasty cocktails, good crowd and cutting-edge music. *Tre Bicchieri Wine Store & Tasting Bar* (Cobanija 3, Sarajevo) has a wide menu of Italian wines plus a relaxing atmosphere.

The old town is lined with lively dance bars where you can mix and mingle with the locals, as well as other tourists and night owls. *Baghdad Café* (Bazardzani 4, Sarajevo) is one of the more popular choices across from Hacienda restaurant, along with many other dance clubs that stay open late on weekends.

Other areas of Bosnia and Herzegovina have a lively nightlife, too. Banja Luka has cool bars, while breweries can be found in cities such as Bihac. Mostar has a selection of nice Old Town lounge bars including *Ali Baba's Cave* (Old Town, Mostar), while Neum's beach scene is more low-key and geared towards families. Winemaking is a longstanding tradition for locals, dating as far back as Roman times. Popular regional drinks and spirits made from fruits are good. Try *sljivovica*, a plum brandy or *ioza*, a clear brandy.

### Dining and Cuisine in Bosnia and Herzegovina

All urban centers in Bosnia and Herzegovina have top-quality restaurants serving not only traditional cuisine, but international fares like Italian, Vietnamese, and Mediterranean. In addition to grilled meats and stews served *jagnjetina* and *bosanski ionac*-style, local specialties like *burek* and *cevapcici* are also worth lining up for. *Cevapcici* is the tasty local sausage made from beef and lamb, while *burek* is a type of pie (either meat or cheese) made with filo dough or pita. The old town in Sarajevo is bursting with shops that sell *burek* and other varieties of the pastry like *zeljanica*, *krompirusa*, and *tikvinica*.

When in the capital, simply follow your nose and you'll find a great restaurant. *Bambus* (Ferhadija 32, Sarajevo), right in the central shopping district, is a good choice for quality food at a reasonable price. If you are looking for traditional Bosnian food, head to *Bsanska Kuca* (Bravadziluk 3, Bascarsija), which is known for its veal broth (*muckalica*) served indoors or outdoors. *Vegehana* (Ferhadija 39,

Sarajevo) is another local favorite, as is *Park Princeva* (Iza Hrida br. 7, Sarajevo). Slightly more expensive, it is worth the extra convertible mark for its elevated location where guests can enjoy scenic views of the city.

There are many Turkish restaurants in Sarajevo, as well. *Inat Kuca* (Veliki Alifakovac 1, Bascarsija) is known for its tasty stews and riverside setting, while *Ottoman Kebap House* (Old Town, Sarajevo) serves up spicier fare. For quality Mexican food in Bosnia and Herzegovina, *Hacienda* (Bazardzani 3, Sarajevo) is your best bet. Frequented by the hip crowd, this trendy place is known for house music, tasty cocktails, and it stays open until early morning.

Delicious vegan choices are available at *Karuzo* (Mehmeda Spahe, Sarajevo), but the place is small, with seating for only 18 people, so allow yourself plenty of time to spare if you want to give it a try. *Moja Mala Kuhinja* (Sarajevo) features live cooking demonstrations and is owned by celebrity chef Muamer Kurtagic.

Outside the capital, both high-end and budget choices are still easy to find, with Banja Luka boasting the cellar-housed *Kazamat* (Tvardjava Kastel, Banja Luka) for excellent three-course meals. Mostar Old Town has the usual array of pizzas and grills, as well as places serving traditional Bosnian fare. Seaside Neum mostly features grill houses, many of which serve sardines.

## Shopping and Leisure

Bosnia and Herzegovina is not big on shopping though there are some interesting places to get traditional items like handmade carpets, woodcarvings, ceramics, brass coffee pots, embroidery, tapestries, wool, wines, and leather. Markets and fairs are common in towns and cities where all kinds of artisans sell their handiwork. Fresh and cooked food is everywhere, along with jewelry, clothing and souvenirs. The central Bosnia region and the town of Visoko are popular for quality leatherwork.

There are large shopping centers and malls in the cities, but it is more fun to visit bazaars and boutique shops. The souk area in Sarajevo is a good place to shop for souvenirs and local goods. A popular shoemaker known as Andar can be found near the Emperor's mosque in the capital who sells handmade shoes and sandals. Next to Gazi Husrev-beg Mosque is a fair trade store known as BHcrafts which has handmade products from accessories to clothing and home decor.

Haggling is acceptable in most markets and expect inflated prices if you are a foreigner. Bringing a local Bosnian with you to help get a better deal.

## Spas in Bosnia and Herzegovina

Bosnia and Herzegovina is gifted with beautiful mountain rivers and thermal springs. Many of these are in the process of modernization, but you can still find natural spas throughout the country. Spa tourism is a big part of Sarajevo, the ski center of Bjelasnica/Igman and areas like Fojnica, Banja Luka, and Teslic. Treatments are more reasonably priced than other European cities.

# Transportation

## Bosnia and Herzegovina Taxis and Car Rental

Cities in Bosnia and Herzegovina are well served by taxis, but be careful not to fall victim to scams, especially when picking one up from the airport or major train or bus depot. It is best to have a map handy so you can ascertain you are being taken to the right place instead of a more expensive trip out of the way. Several taxi companies operate within the cities and *Sarajevo Taxi* (1515) and *SaraevoTaxiService* (+387-77-731-333) are reliable. Those traveling around Mostar have fewer choices, but *Mostar Taxi Adis* (+387-61-652-149) is dependable.

Renting a car is possible, but don't expect smooth traffic and pleasant driving, especially within the cities. Major car rental companies like *Europcar* (+387-33-760-360) and *Budget* (+387-33-766-670) have a presence in the Bosnia. There are also local providers in Mostar, Banja

Luka, and Sarajevo, including *CITO Car Rental* (+387-33-769-890) and *Adriatic rent-a-car* (+387-36-580-021). Driving yourself is a good way to explore the country, especially the more remote destinations. However, mountainous terrains can be tricky to navigate, and gas stations are hard to come by. There is a constant landmine threat, especially in the countryside, so it is best not to wander away from paved roads.

**Bosnia and Herzegovina Water Taxis**

There are ferries between Neum and neighboring cities on the Adriatic. Inland lakes and rivers provide possibilities for boat travel between cities though many services are privately run. Alternatively, you can hitchhike your way round the country. Friendly locals will be more than happy to help you, although public transportation is still your safest bet.

**Bosnia and Herzegovina Trains and Buses**

A reliable tram network serves the city center of Sarajevo, making it easy to get around. Bus lines run by small private companies travel to nearby towns and cities. Take note that if you purchase a return ticket for a line that is served by two or more companies, your ticket will only be honored by the company it was bought from.

Train services are beginning to catch on with the growing demand for rail networks though many lines are still in the process of rebuilding from damages caused by the war. Services can be infrequent and the ride slow. However, train travel is rewarding, thanks to the scenic mountains, especially between Mostar and Sarajevo. Regular trips are also available from Sarajevo to Banja Luka and from Tuzla to Banja Luka.

## Airports

### Sarajevo International Airport

Sarajevo International Airport is the main air gateway into Bosnia and Herzegovina. It is situated in the Butmir suburb, 3.7 miles from the city's train station. The airport is a hub for flagship carrier BH Airlines, which connects to major cities throughout Europe, including Copenhagen, Prague, Skopje, Amsterdam, and Istanbul. From these, it is possible to get connections to many US airports.

The main international airport in Bosnia has a two-level passenger terminal with a spacious central hall. The modern building is fully equipped with passenger amenities, including restaurants, snack bars, a duty-free shop, a VIP lounge, some newsstands, a bank, and a currency exchange office. A transit desk is available in the waiting area, while car rental can be found on the ground floor.

Unfortunately, there is no direct public transportation from the airport to downtown. Taxi fares are regulated, but they tend to be expensive for such a short distance. You will also find car rental providers National, Hertz, Sixt, Budget, Europcar, and Dollar.

### Tulza International Airport

Open from 6:00 a.m. to 8:00 p.m., Tulza's airport serves just one carrier, Sky Airlines. The single commercial route is to Antalya, Turkey. Facilities at the airport are good and include a restaurant and snack bar, currency exchange and a post office. Transport into Tulza is provided by buses and taxis.

### Banja Luka International Airport

Located just over 10 miles from Banja Luka's main railway station, this airport serves Bosnia and Herzegovina's second city and surrounds. A single carrier, B&H Airlines, offers one route to Zurich, Switzerland four times a week. It is possible to arrange for a rental car to be dropped off at the airport through Banja Luka suppliers like Rentacar Omega.

## Travel Tips

**Language:** Bosnian, Croatian, and Serbian are the three official languages spoken here. They are collectively known as Serbo-Croatian since they are virtually the same, with a few vocabulary differences.

The language is written in Cyrillic and Latin. Street signs, especially in Republika Srpska, are in Cyrillic, which is why it is smart to have a Serbian-English dictionary handy along with a phrasebook. Many locals speak good English, especially the younger generation and a number of people know German. However, it is best to learn basic Bosnian phrases to be able to tell your cab driver where to go and to ask for directions.

**Currency:** The official currency in Bosnia and Herzegovina is the convertible mark (KM). Currently, two sets of banknotes are accepted throughout the country. Avoid paying with 100 KM bills in small shops, as they might not have enough change for such a large bill. It is easy to find ATMs in the cities, and most machines accept Maestro or Visa cards. Credit cards are of little use in the country since only large establishments and brand name hotels accept them.

**Time:** GMT +1

**Electricity:** Bring a voltage converter if you are using devices that do not accept 230 Volts of current at 50 cycles per second. A plug adapter may also be necessary, as sockets used in most hotels and throughout the country are Europlug and Schuko types.

**Communications:** The country code for Bosnia and Herzegovina is +387. Phone booths can be found in post offices and bus stations, but they don't accept coins, meaning you will have to buy a pre-paid calling card to use them. Calls from hotels are generally expensive, but mobile phone networks are a cheaper alternative. You can buy cheap prepaid SIM cards at the airport.

**Duty-free:** Works of art cannot be exported from the country. However, duty-free goods are available from different tax-free shops in the international airports of Mostar, Sarajevo, and Tuzla. Additionally, you can enter the country with up to 200 cigarettes (or 200g of tobacco or 20 cigars), one liter of wine or spirits, a bottle of perfume, and gifts not exceeding US $98.90 in value without incurring customs duty.

**Tourist Office:** Tourism Association of Bosnia and Herzegovina PR Office: +387-33-252-901 or http://www.bhtourism.ba/eng/.

**Consulates in Bosnia and Herzegovina:** United States Consulate, Sarajevo: +387-33-445-700 British Consulate, Sarajevo: +387-33-282-200 French Consulate, Sarajevo: +387-33-282-050 Greek Consulate, Sarajevo: +387-33-211-794 Macedonia Consulate, Sarajevo: +387 33-810-760

**Emergency:** Police: 122 Fire: 123 Emergency: 124 Roadside Assistance and Road Conditions: 1282 International Phone Operator: 1201

International Directory Enquires: 1183 Local Directory Enquires: 1182
Time: 125

## Visas and Vaccinations

Generally, EU citizens and neighboring nationalities can enter Bosnia and Herzegovina with only a passport or a national identity card, and stay for up to 90 days. Foreign nationals from North, Central, and South American territories, including the United States and a handful of Asian countries, can likewise enter the country visa-free for up to 90 days with a passport. Tourists of other nationalities will have to acquire a visa from the Bosnian and Herzegovinian consulate or embassy in their respective country.

**Health and Safety**
Bosnia and Herzegovina is a delightful and safe country to explore. However, you should take certain precautions. Your travel and health insurance should be in place before traveling. It is best to get immunized against tuberculosis and hepatitis B, and to prevent against tick-borne encephalitis by checking carefully after forest walks. Tap water is potable and of high quality throughout the country. Food hygiene is also of high standard, even in small shops in the old town of Sarajevo.

Bosnia and Herzegovina is one of the safest places to visit in Europe. However, there are threats of land mines in remote country areas and abandoned villages. Stay away from taped areas, former confrontation lines and rural regions not frequented by travelers. Violence and even petty crimes are virtually nonexistent and visitors can freely walk without worrying about their safety at any time of the day. Just use common sense when returning to your hotel at night.

## Weather

Bosnia and Herzegovina enjoys a pleasant mix of central European and Mediterranean climates, so expect hot summers and chilly winters. In elevated areas, snowfall can last until April, and typical winter temperatures average 28°F. Hot spells during summer bring temperatures up to 80°F. The country experiences variable weather conditions as a result of its hilly and mountainous terrain.

Avoid the cold months if you are a hiker, unless you are up for a challenging, chilly ascent and tricky, snow-covered trails. Ski resorts are open at least four months a year. When planning your wardrobe, be sure to bring warm clothes and a jacket during winter and lightweight shirts for summer. If you are planning to visit the wetter and colder northern towns and higher altitude regions, it is best to pack for cold temperatures regardless of the time of year.

**Best Time to Visit Bosnia and Herzegovina**

Bosnia and Herzegovina is a great place to visit any time of the year. Warm summer seasons see plenty of hikers, nature trippers, and adventure seekers flocking to the mountains for fun in the sun. Winter and fall attract ski enthusiasts looking for Alpine adventures. The country looks beautiful in spring, when the fields are in bloom and temperatures are pleasant throughout the day.

Nature enthusiasts should save their Bosnia holidays for the months of October and November, when the forests are a lovely mix of colors. Skiers will best enjoy the slopes from January to March. Some fantastic Olympic ski areas can be found in the Jahorina, Igman and Bjelasnica mountains. You should, however, anticipate crowds during this time. Be smart when planning logistics and itineraries and make sure to have advance reservations for hotels closest to the ski lift.

# Holidays and Festivals

Whatever time of the year you choose to visit Bosnia and Herzegovina, you'll never run out of things to do. The locals have an innate love for festivities and celebrations, so it is impossible to get bored. Fascinating Bosnia and Herzegovina holiday traditions and Olympic-style competitions are held in different regions throughout the year, along with countless religious celebrations.

**International Sarajevo Winter Festival:** This festival began in 1984 and has since grown to become one of the most anticipated events in Bosnia and Herzegovina. Often held in the month of February, art exhibits from different parts of the world compete for the highest title possible, the *Sestoaprilska Negarda Sarajeva*.

**Banja Luka Choir Gathering:** Held during April or May, this annual gathering has a series of programs that features some of the most angelic voices in Bosnia and Herzegovina.

**Kid's Festival:** If you are planning a family vacation, try your best to catch the Kid's Festival, which is held during June. It is a great way to get children acquainted with the different types of art and to keep them entertained with workshops and fun. Performances feature jugglers, dancers and magicians.

**Bascarsija Nights:** One of the most popular cultural events in Sarajevo, the month-long festival of Bascarsija Nights features some 40 to 50 different events that honor the rich culture of Bosnia. It is marked by different children's programs, literary events, film showings, classical music, and even opera and ballet.

**Summer on the Vrabas:** Every year in July, this traditional celebration offers a unique mix of athletic competitions and cultural programs. It is held near Kastel Fortress and attracts athletes and artists who are eager to share their skills and display their abilities through presentations, racing and many other activities.

**Sarajevo Film Festival:** The Sarajevo Fim festival is held annually in August. Long and short regional films from a wide variety of genres are shown (some for free). It also serves as a huge venue for artists from all over the world to meet and share their passion for the arts.

**Banja Luka Summer Games:** Held in August, the Summer Games draw crowds from all over the world and Bosnia. Just like Summer on the Vrabas, this event takes place around the historic town of Kastel.

**Jazzfest Sarajevo:** Held in November, Jazzfest Sarajevo is the best place to enjoy Bosnia and Herzegovina's rich music scene. The city's café culture is at its liveliest.

www.ingramcontent.com/pod-product-compliance
Lightning Source LLC
Chambersburg PA
CBHW021111080526
44587CB00010B/473